Backroads of British Columbia

Backroads of British Columbia

by Liz & Jack Bryan

SUNFLOWER BOOKS
Vancouver, British Columbia, Canada

ISBN 0-88894-090-4 (Cloth)
ISBN 0-88894-091-2 (Paperback)

Printed and bound in Canada by
EVERGREEN PRESS LIMITED,
Vancouver, British Columbia.

Contents

Introduction

Travellers who drive only the highways miss the best of British Columbia. Highways are built for speed, and take, if not the shortest, then the easiest routes to reach their destinations. But between the highways, wandering off towards obscure settlements, climbing mountains or following rivers apparently just for the hell of it, are other roads, less travelled and less easy to travel. These are the backroads — hundreds of them — mostly not shown on tourist maps and generally ignored because they offer no paved surfaces, no tourist comforts. Better than any highways, the backroads lead to the lonely places of B.C. where you can experience, if only for a brief time, the great challenge of the wilderness.

Few areas have so much wild land so easy of access as British Columbia. Purists may argue that once a road has been put through, even a winding cart track, then the land is wild no longer. And perhaps they are right. But we could take you to places where Man has been settled for over 100 years. He has built roads and cabins, worked the land with his plough, diverted little creeks to water his scrimping patches of hay, suffered the cold of winter and the heat of summer. He has put his mark indelibly on the land. And yet we know you will find these places, as we do, perhaps among the loneliest and wildest on earth. Man is not an intruder here; his life has meshed with the wilderness; he suffers its pain and its joy, and his cycle of birth and death and renewal is seen, after all, as only part of the greater rhythms of the universe.

The backroads of B.C. are tangible links with the history of Man and his influence on the B.C. wilderness. They follow Indian trails, fur-trade routes, crude roads hacked hastily from the bush by men lusting for gold. They are the routes of stage coaches and wagon trains and railways, ranchers driving their cattle to market, and loggers hauling out giants from the virgin forests. They all are, or were, working roads. They were built for a purpose and their importance in the opening up of the province was immense. Some lead to places derelict and forlorn — old logging camps, mining towns that failed, homesteads that were abandoned, towns that declined in importance, usually because the railway went elsewhere. Some have been bypassed by newer, faster roads, and faded with the tourist trade. Whatever their reason for being, the backroads pry deeply into the soul of B.C. to reveal much of its essentially frontier spirit. And driving on them will give you not only views of some of the most beautiful scenery on earth, but a knowledge of the land itself, its contours, geography, vegetation, climate, history — and how Man is shaping it to his purpose. When a political decision is to be made — a river to be dammed or an oil refinery built — you will have something to say about it.

If you drive the backroads often, as we do, you will notice many changes, most of them sad ones. A quiet lakeshore may be subdivided for summer cottages; a new power line may ruin a splendid view; the dirt road may be blacktopped, bringing in more people; or a forest fire may have ravaged the area. But the saddest change of all is the disappearance of some of the old historic landmarks. A lovely group of old log barns and corrals beside the Cariboo Wagon Road above

Lillooet was simply not there when we drove by one spring; we never did discover what had happened to them. Another landmark, a stern old pioneer homestead in a Bridesville field, was pulled down almost in front of our eyes. It was there one week, gone the next. Only a pile of shattered timbers remained.

Much of B.C.'s past is disappearing, not only because few people care about it but because the buildings themselves are made of wood, and will eventually rot and collapse unless protected. You can't really blame the farmer for clearing them off his land. We decided to give photographs of some of the vanished landmarks in this book, to show people what we have lost.

Backroads of B.C. is not a travel book in the usual sense. It ignores huge areas of interest to the general tourist and covers only portions of southern B.C. It is not a nature book, though all the roads described are good places to find wildflowers, birds, deer, bear, mushrooms, fish etc. And it is not intended to be a history book, although some of the roads follow historic routes or lead to historic places; there are Indian pictographs, stories of highwaymen and buried treasure, miners who struck it rich, ghost towns and ghost railways and always the pioneer settlers. Much of the province's history happened along these roads and we have tried to include as much of it as possible. We hope historians will not find too many faults, although we are certain they will find gaps.

We like backroads, because, being older, they are narrow, winding, unpaved — and blissfully free of traffic even during holiday weekends. We drive them slowly, for the pure pleasure of the scenery, stopping for photographs whenever we please and enjoying the quiet of the countryside. Because traffic is light (sometimes non-existent as we discovered once when our car broke down) the birdwatching is particularly good. And early morning and twilight are the best times of day for other forms of wildlife; we have seen deer, bear, moose, beaver, coyote, marmot, mountain sheep, porcupine, all kinds of creatures. Wildflowers are splendid in spring and summer in all the different biotic zones, from semi-desert to alpine meadow, which the backroads traverse.

Often the roads themselves are of interest enough, at least for the first time; but you will find that all lead to areas deserving of closer exploration, and many need to be visited several times before their appeal is fully realized. The Chilliwack River Valley is one such area; you can return there every weekend for a whole summer and still find new places to explore. Hiking, birding, camping, fishing, boating, even gold-panning — the backroads make them all possible.

We hope you enjoy them as much as we do.

Vancouver
September 1975

It has been 2½ years since this book was written and one must expect that some of the roads will have changed. Crooked ways will be straightened, surfaces made either better or worse than they were, perhaps even paved, encouraging speedier traffic and diminishing some of the old appeal. And undoubtedly more of the buildings, our visible history, will have disappeared under the weight of winter snows or impatient bulldozers. But by and large, with the possible exception of Hat Creek, none of the roads described here should have changed enough to make the journeys no longer worthwhile. Certainly, the reasons for writing about the roads in the first place — the history and beauty of the countryside through which they pass — are still every bit as valid now as they ever were.

So go carefully, expect changes, some for the worse, some for the better, convert the miles to kilometers — and have a good time.

April 1978

A Word of Advice

Backroads are not for everyone. The rough dirt roads are bumpy and uncomfortable; they are steep and winding and call for cautious driving. Conditions are uncertain — road surfaces change from year to year, or even from day to day. In summer, dust will billow up and seep through the most tightly sealed of cars to settle on your hair, your clothes, your camera. In spring, the dust will likely be a quagmire, or you could run into a snowbank (we have done this as late as June on a mountain road), or the road may be washed away by a flooding creek or covered by a rock slide. Always check on the conditions of the road before you start — the nearest service station should know — or be prepared to turn back.

Because so much of B.C. is forest, backroad drivers must be prepared for long stretches of woods, which some people find boring or claustrophobic, particularly the tight pickets of the Cariboo jackpines. But after miles of being shut in by forest, even the humblest meadow clearing, lake or barn will seem doubly sweet.

Jolting dirt roads are not good for automobiles. Your shock absorbers and springs will get a good workout, your tires will wear more quickly and flying gravel will pockmark the best paint and could even crack the windshield. If the car breaks down, be prepared for a long wait or a long hike to fetch help. Remember the B.C. Automobile Association will not cover towing charges once you have left the highway.

Backroads fall into several categories. Some are wide and straight and flat; others are steep, narrow tracks navigable only by a four-wheel drive. Discussed here are only those roads that in the normal course of events can be driven easily by the average family automobile. We have travelled all these personally, on several occasions, at different times of year in a variety of cars, from small European to large automatic American models. We found definite advantages in the standard shift and decided that perhaps the most critical factor is high clearance.

Before you embark on a backroad, make sure your car is in good repair, with a spare tire inflated and checked. Carry extra water for drinking and radiator troubles, but spare gasoline only if your car is extraordinarily wasteful. To travel on any of the backroads in this book, all you need to do is fill your gas tank before you leave the highway. Some of the longer backroads have gas stations en route.

Pack a picnic lunch (few of the roads have any services). Wear stout shoes for hiking and old, comfortable clothes. Bring binoculars, fishing rods, flower identification guides and, in summer, mosquito repellent.

Do not trespass on private land. It's safer to ask permission. Some of the roads pass through rangeland. Be sure to close all gates securely behind you. Respect the wilderness and do not spoil it for others. Remove all litter, douse your picnic fires well, cut no trees or flowers, play no loud radios, drive no noisy trailbikes. Help keep the backroads of B.C. as beautiful as they are now.

The maps in this book are intended for general orientation only. The backroad routes are emphasized and all other roads, highways and dirt tracks alike, are drawn in the same style. Do not go without a large-scale provincial government map which shows all the backroads. Recommended are the National Topographic System maps published by the B.C. Department of Lands, Forests and Water Resources. Best scale is 1 inch to 2 miles. The maps are available for a small sum from government agent's offices.

(Many of the stories and photographs in this book first appeared in Western Living magazine.)

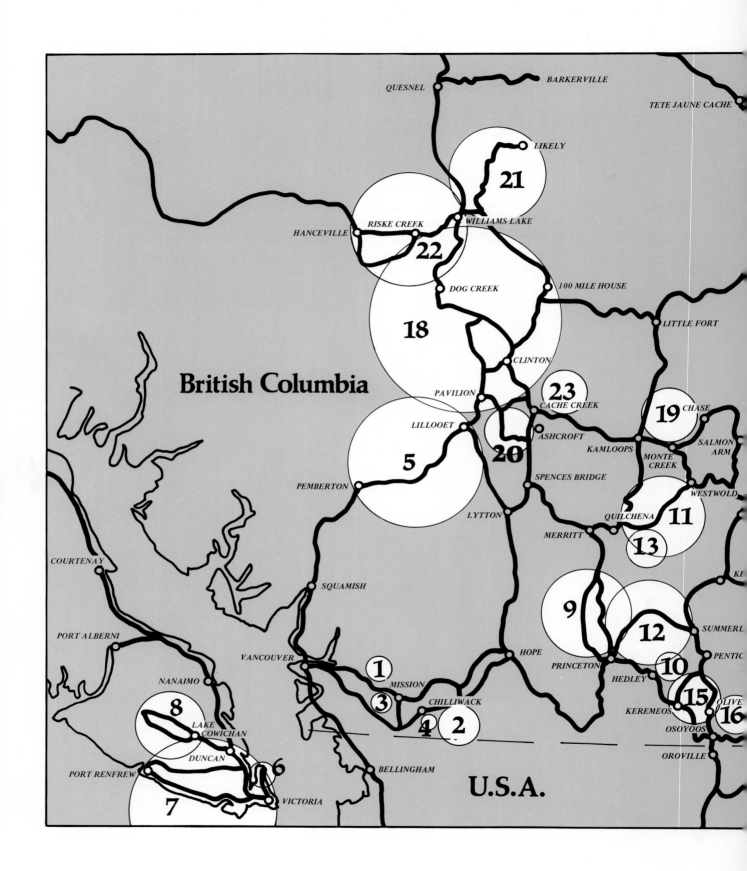

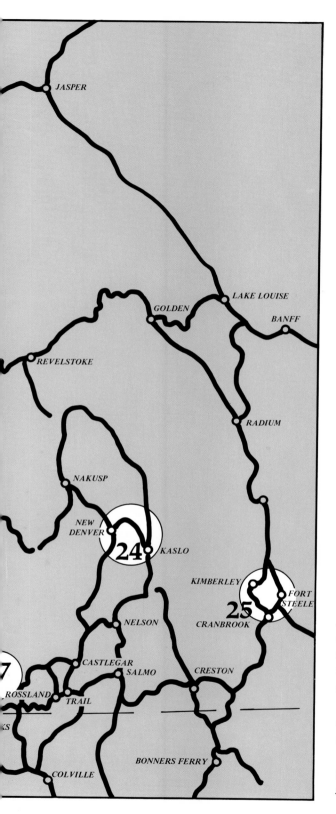

JASPER

LAKE LOUISE

GOLDEN

BANFF

REVELSTOKE

RADIUM

NAKUSP

NEW
DENVER

24

KASLO

KIMBERLEY

FORT
STEELE

25

NELSON

CRANBROOK

7

CASTLEGAR

CRESTON

ROSSLAND

SALMO

TRAIL

BONNERS FERRY

COLVILLE

This sketch map of British Columbia gives approximate locations of the 25 Backroad Tours featured in this book. It should be used in conjunction with a good road map and detailed topographic maps of the tour areas.

The book, as you can see, covers only some of the backroads of southern B.C. We hope to cover some of the roads of the north in a subsequent edition.

TOUR 1

Pitt Polder Rambles

Across the dewy fields, mists rise like wraiths from the ditches and the murky shadows of cows browse the morning grass. A lacy line of trees stands stark against the sky and spiders' webs glisten. Unless you have noticed the pale line of mountains to the North you might well believe it is Holland. The land is flat and dyked, threaded with water channels. The farms are neat, with an orderly spacing and the quality of light, the richness in the grass and the cry of gulls stir strong memories of the North Sea. This is Pitt Polder, a tranquil pocket of countryside surprisingly close to the bustle of Vancouver. Here, on land reclaimed from the floods (the definition of the Dutch word polder) are pleasant backroads for a Sunday drive and dyke paths for brisk family hikes. Or you can launch a boat on Pitt Lake and fish for cutthroat and Dolly Varden trout.

How did a Dutch polder find its way to British Columbia? The Pitt River, the Fraser's last major tributary, drains from Pitt Lake, a huge, mountain-rimmed reservoir swollen in spring by melting snows. At the drainage end of the lake is a wedge of land scoured flat by ancient glaciers except for three small bony hillocks. This flat land, only five feet above sea level and a mere two feet higher than the Pitt River high tide, was flooded every spring; the hillocks became islands in a marshy waterland. Early Fraser Valley settlers spurned the area in favor of higher, safer ground. Some attempts were made to embank the land but none were successful, and the marshes remained for the waterbirds alone until 1948 when a Dutch immigrant, Dr. Jan Blom, came to the area. For 25 years, the land that is now Pitt Polder had been a private duck-hunting reserve, the marshes protected from inundation by a crude dyke. That spring, the waters of the Pitt burst the dyke, covering the marsh with several feet of water. Even the duck hunters gave up in despair. But Dr. Blom knew the land could be reclaimed. He took out an option on the area, had engineering studies done and interested Dutch investment in the project. The following year, he founded a company, Pitt Polder Ltd., to empolder the marshes and manage the new-found farmland. The older dykes were rebuilt 16 feet above sea level and an enclosed system of inner dykes was constructed. Diversion channels caught mountain run-off water and pumps, capable of moving 85,000 gallons of water a minute, were put into action. Some 5,000 acres of the floodlands were successfully reclaimed.

Local people remained skeptical of the project. There were old wives' tales about the dire effect of mountain water on pasture and old fears for the savagery of B.C. rivers in flood. Laborers recruited for the dyke building turned out to be mainly Dutch immigrants, and many of them later applied for leases on the farmsteads established in the dyked area south of Sturgeon Slough. Pitt Polder became a Dutch colony, although that was never the intent, and the names you see today on mailboxes in the area are mostly still of Dutch origin. European cows, Holsteins and Guernseys, populate dairy meadows that look so much like Holland. Beside Rannie Road, north of Sturgeon Slough, the Netherlands Overseas Nurseries grows ornamental trees and shrubs. At one time, daffodils

The magic of a misty morning at Pitt Polder: a line of half-denuded trees like lace against the sky; pendants of dew on spider's webs and thistles.

Cows munch the foggy
grass, facing into the sunrise.
Then the sun breaks through,
mists vanish and mountains
etch their shadows on the sky.

were planted in the polderfields, but these did not flourish. Instead, under the shadow of the mountain along the eastern edge of the polder, 100 acres are planted with blueberries.

Today, though the polders are productive dairy farms, the area has a wild appealing quality. Waterfowl frequent the marshy areas of the north end; hawks patrol the fields; great blue heron fish the sloughs and riverbanks; beavers thwack their tails in the ditches; and in spring the sandhill cranes return to mate and build their nests. Pitt Polder is one of the few areas in B.C. where you can see these great birds, bigger than a heron and brown rather than grey, with rosy crowns. Bird watching in general is excellent here, and the high dyke paths provide dry walking even in winter.

In 1972 the British Columbia government acquired for greenbelt the northernmost 3,000 acres of the polder area, including the boggy nesting sites of the sandhill cranes. This area, plus 1,500 acres of existing wildlife reserve at the end of the lake, will be managed to provide protected wildlife habitat as well as public recreation. A limited amount of dyking and drainage is proposed but the vast sphagnum moss bog, with its jungle of swamp laurel and huckleberry, will be left undisturbed for the cranes, which, in 1975, numbered five nesting pairs and eight singles.

To reach the Polders of the Pitt, drive east from Vancouver along Highway No. 7 (Lougheed Highway) north of the Fraser River. Cross the Coquitlam River and then the humped back bridge over the Pitt, at the Wild Duck Inn. Turn left immediately over the bridge onto the Dewdney Trunk Road. From here there are several ways to go. One of the best turns north onto Harris Road over the Alouette River, then east onto McNeil Road which meanders around steep Sheridan Hill to join Rannie Road, the main road through the Polder to Pitt Lake. You can also continue east on Dewdney until you reach Neaves Road, the southern extension of Rannie Road, for the long straight drive north to public boat launching at the lake's southern end.

The polder areas to the south are best explored on foot or bicycle along the tops of the dykes, which, forbidden to cars or motorbikes, offer a rare solitude. If you want a simple but longish hike, park your car near the north side of Sturgeon Slough bridge and walk the dyke west along the slough to join the river. The dyke road follows the curve of the river around to meet the northern end of Rannie Road, which leads you back to your car. For shorter circuits take one of the connecting roads back to Rannie Road. A shorter loop walk is made possible by following the Alouette dyke from the bridge on Harris Road west to the Pitt, then up the river to meet Harris Road again. And a longer Y-shaped circuit (about nine miles) follows the dykes from the Harris bridge east along the Alouette River's north arm, crossing over and returning via the south arm dykes to the starting point.

TOUR 2

Beside the Wild Chilliwack

I t's a valley for hikers, for fishermen, for lovers of the deep jungled forest with its ferns and mushrooms and mosses. It's a valley well laced with roads for back-lane dawdlers, yet wild enough to please those in search of solitude. For summer, there is even a long, cool lake. But best of all, the Chilliwack River valley provides some of the most spectacular mountain views on the Lower Mainland. The 8,000-foot massifs of Slesse, Rexford and the Border Peaks rear up steeply above the valley, astoundingly high and frosty above the forest's deep greens.

Before Europeans came to the Fraser Valley in search of fur and gold, all this was Indian country. The name Chilliwack or Chilukweyuk means "Valley of Many Streams". The Salish Indians who lived here belonged to the Stalo or river tribe for their lives depended on the rivers which not only brought them salmon but provided transportation routes through the dense forests and mountains. In the Chilliwack valley were several ancient villages, with both the plank houses of the Coast and the pit houses or "keekwillie holes" of the Interior — as if this was the boundary between Coast and Interior influences. Today, unless you know exactly where to look, all trace of these villages has vanished.

Indian trails ran along both sides of the Chilliwack River, up the major tributaries and over the high mountain divides to the south and east. The first trappers and later, miners en route to the Fraser and Cariboo goldfields used the same trails. The loggers, who came later still, used them too. Today, backroads up the Chilliwack are mostly logging roads, except for one stretch north of the river that was built by the army. They are good for excursions at most times of year, though spring provides the loveliest views of mountains still thickly covered with snow and fall has the advantage of color in the trees, mists on the lake and the wild bounty of mushrooms. The river is famous for its steelhead, best from November to May, while spring brings cutthroat, rainbows and Dolly Varden. Mountain hikes are usually best in summer, when the snows have gone from the alpine meadows.

The Chilliwack River rises in Washington state and flows north into B.C. where it immediately forms a fat finger of a lake some five miles long. Then the river meanders westwards towards the Fraser. Thirty miles downstream from the lake it is bridged by the highway connecting the city of Chilliwack with Cultus Lake. West of the bridge, the river is known as the Vedder. Before flood protection measures and the draining of Sumas Lake, the Chilliwack turned north at the bridge site. Then it was diverted and canalized and its new course was named the Vedder after one of the area's earliest homesteaders, Volkert Vedder, who arrived here in 1858 from California.

The settlement at the bridge is called Vedder Crossing, headquarters for the annual Boxing Day Steelhead Derby. Here, too, the Canadian Armed Forces have a military base. The Royal Engineers (or Sappers, as they are called) have been long in B.C. Stationed at first near New Westminster (at Sapperton), they not only surveyed this earliest of the mainland cities, but also constructed two

*The Chilliwack Valley is
beautiful at every season.
Opposite page: Slesse
Creek chatters clear and loud
beneath the snow spires of
the Border Peaks in
spring. Above: The forests
are dark and jungled,
luxuriant with moss. Left:
Frosty edges on autumn leaves.*

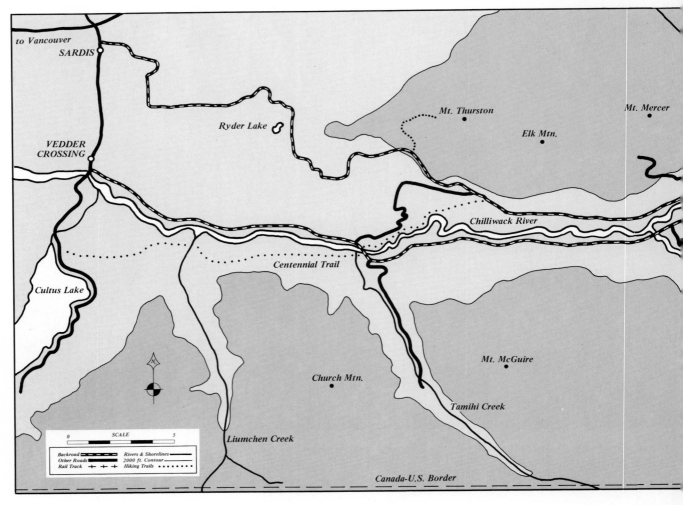

very important roads, the Cariboo Wagon Road to Barkerville and a good part of the Dewdney Trail. Traces of the latter, known as the Engineers' Road, can still be seen beside today's highway through Manning Park. The Canadian Military Engineers' museum on the Chilliwack base gives glimpses of the province's early military history with displays of artifacts and memorabilia, documents and old photographs. Another exhibit is a diorama of the Battle of Waterloo, with 1,500 hand-painted lead soldiers. The museum is open on Sunday afternoons all year and every afternoon during the school summer vacation.

The backroads of the Chilliwack begin at Vedder Crossing. To get there, drive east along Highway No. 1 (the Trans-Canada) beyond Abbotsford and take the Sardis-Cultus Lake turnoff. Drive through Sardis and the military camp to the Chilliwack-Vedder bridge, turn left and head upriver. Sports fishermen will know this spot well; at any weekend you will see them along the banks or standing hip-deep in the swirling water.

Eight miles or so along the way, a side road branches left to Slesse Park where a cairn commemorates the crash of a passenger airliner on Mount Slesse back in the 1950s. It was a foggy night. The plane simply disappeared into the mountain wilderness and the wreckage and the bodies of all aboard were not discovered until the following spring. A short distance beyond, the road crosses the river and veers left to follow the south bank of the Chilliwack. A road coming in from the right leads back along the river to Cultus Lake and Vedder Crossing. Here, too, the Centennial Trail crosses the river. This trail, a Youth Hostels Association Centennial project, goes all the way

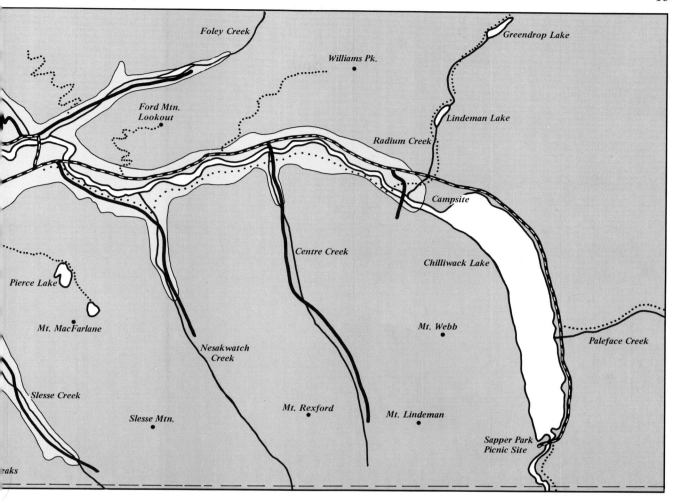

from New Westminster to Manning Park, mostly following old Indian and Hudson's Bay Co. trails. It cuts into the valley from Cultus Lake and runs in opposition to the main road — when the trail is south of the river, the road is north — and they cross over on or near the same bridges. The bridges thus provide good starting points for short hikes along the trail. Start at one bridge and arrange vehicle pickup at the next.

It's a little over five miles from Slesse Park to the bridge over Slesse Creek, and in between you pass the entrance to one of three forestry correction camps in the valley. Just over Slesse bridge is one of the best of the mountain views. Stop where a road comes in from the right and look back to the incredible spires of the Border Peaks, Canadian and American, which straddle the international boundary. The best time for photography is early morning because the peaks face east. Slesse Creek marks the boundary of fishing on the Chilliwack. The river is closed from the creek mouth to the lake except for a limited open season, usually in July. Slesse Creek itself is also closed to fishing, but it's a beautiful stream, clear and swift-flowing, with many good picnic spots and excellent mountain views. A rough road follows Slesse all the way to the boundary, providing access to an old gold mine on the slopes of Red Mountain. The ore was rawhided down, then packed out by horses. Halfway house for the pack train was near Slesse Park, though today no trace remains. The road is now mostly used for logging, and some sluice box mining for gold is continued in the upper valley. Hikers also use the road to reach the Slesse Mountain trail, but this is a trip for experts.

A mile after crossing Slesse Creek (Slesse is Salish for "fangs"), a forest nursery on the left

*Chilliwack Lake in hazy
shades of blue from fall slash-
burning smoke. In spring,
pussy willows are hung with
golden pollen; in fall, alder and
cottonwood bronze the
lakeshore.*

marks the area of the Pierce Lake trail. A five-mile hike leads steeply to the lake and its nearby derelict cabin and up to mine diggings on the lip of a second, higher lake. Allow a full day for the return trip. Two miles farther, the main road makes its second Chilliwack crossing and from then on it stays on the north bank all the way to the lake. Two more hiking trails start from the following section of road. The first goes up to a forestry lookout on Ford Mountain and the second, a few miles farther along, to Williams Peak along a scenic ridge. Allow five and seven hours respectively for each trip. From the Williams trail near the Centre Creek forestry camp it's about six miles to the lake. The Centennial Trail crosses the river just before the lake, where there is a cluster of summer cabins and a youth hostel, and follows Post Creek up to Lindeman and Greendrop Lakes, then over the divide into the Silverhope Valley, south of Hope. Lindeman Lake, reached in an hour from the valley, is an excellent family excursion.

At Chilliwack Lake, the road forks, the right branch going to the campsite and on to the beach and boat launching site. Many people make this their final destination. But if you keep to the left road you can continue along the lakeshore all the way to the head of the lake, another five miles or so. This section is narrow and well used by logging trucks so it is recommended driving only at weekends. The road may be gated at Paleface Creek, about two-thirds of the way down, but if it is open, as it should be on weekends, continue through to lake's end where there are extensive beaches, excellent fishing and even a picnic site built by the Chilliwack Engineers at Sapper Park, across Victoria Bridge. Here the Sappers have built an iron gateway with plaques denoting that this was the campsite of the Sappers when they surveyed the international boundary back in the 1850s.

A trail leads up the east side of the upper Chilliwack River to the U.S. border and beyond, linking up with Whatcom Pass. It was over this pass in the days of the Gold Rush that American miners came en route to the Fraser. They trekked this way from Whatcom, (now Bellingham) to evade a head tax levied on foreigners by Governor Douglas in Victoria. They "smuggled" themselves in over the mountains, then followed fur and Indian trails down to Chilliwack, or went by way of Post Creek over to Fort Hope. The trail, undoubtedly the one used by the Sappers in the 1850s, passes through some magnificent old forest. It is definitely worth making the two-hour return trip to the border.

To vary the return route to Vedder Crossing, go down the main road over the first river bridge, then take the second turn on the right which may be marked Chipmunk Road. This crosses back over the river onto the old Engineers' Road which leads down the north side of the valley. It's an older and prettier road than the other, with the forest grown back along the edges and with many more deciduous trees. In fall, it's particularly beautiful. In early days there was a logging railway up this side of the river and its roadbed and some traces of old trestle are still to be found in the bush.

Bear left at the first two major forks and stop often to look back at the mountains across the river. Mount Slesse is most impressive from this side. At the third fork, turn right and continue climbing in a general north-westerly direction until you come eventually to Elk View Road in pastoral Ryder Lake (see Backroad No. 4). One last hike is possible before you head for home. About a mile past the third forks, a trail starts up beside a gravel pit to Elk Mountain, a stiff six-mile round trip that is amply rewarded with masses of alpine flowers and wild strawberries in season. The mountain views from the top are panoramic. To return to Vancouver, follow Elk View Road down to the Fraser Valley floor, then head west back to Vedder Road for access to the freeway.

TOUR 3
Through Fraser Valley Fields

The Fraser Valley stretches from Hope a hundred miles to the sea. Its undulating pastures, contained by a tall picket maze of mountains, provide not only natural farmland — some of the richest on earth — but an obvious transportation route. The men of the Hudson's Bay Co. slashed the first recorded trail up the valley, following an Indian route along the Nikomekl and Salmon Rivers to the Fraser where they founded Fort Langley. Later, the Fraser River provided the road for the Gold Rush traffic of the 1880s; paddle-wheelers ran regularly from New Westminster to Yale, calling in at river settlements along the way. Wagon roads brought the farmers' products to market and later, two transcontinental railways sped through the valley.

Today, Trans-Canada Highway No.1 carves an angular swath through valley fields south of the river, bypassing most of the towns and providing a fast exit route for Vancouverites bound for the Okanagan or the Cariboo. The valley itself tends to be forgotten. But it is still a beautiful place, despite suburban encroachment, with a pace as quiet and unhurried as the munching cows in the fields. Highway No.1 allows only tantalizing glimpses of this serenity. To appreciate the valley's charms, you must travel the backroads, stopping often and branching off on foot or bicycle. There is much to see.

On any large scale map of the Fraser Valley you'll discover that the countryside is criss-crossed by little meandering alternatives to the freeway, roads which you can follow to just about any valley destination. This one takes you to Barnston Island, on to Fort Langley, then along the river to Bradner where, in April, the fields are emblazoned with daffodils. The tour covers less than 100 miles, but needs a full day.

Start on Highway 1 heading east from the Port Mann Bridge. Turn off at the third interchange, 176 Street or Clover Valley Road, its older and prettier name. Once off the exit ramp, turn sharp left and cross over the freeway, heading north. The road plunges downhill towards the river for about a mile before meeting 104 Avenue. Turn right onto the Barnston Island ferry landing. Barnston is one of several little silty islands washed up by the Fraser, and it's the only one that is accessible to the public by ferry. Run by the B.C. Department of Highways to service the island residents, it has two components: an open deck barge big enough for three cars, and a jaunty tugboat which noses the barge across the river. The ferry is free and runs on demand, staying at the island dock until called (just honk your horn).

Barnston is small, a fat crescent about three miles long and two miles broad, lying so low in the Fraser that it was always in flood until an encircling dyke was built. Today the dyke is topped by a paved road making it possible to circuit the island by car in a matter of minutes, if speed is your object. But the island needs time to be appreciated. Leave your car on the mainland and cross the ferry as a foot passenger, or bring your bicycle. In winter, the dyke road is dry underfoot and, being high, gives a splendid view over the fields and river. In spring and summer, unpaved lanes, winding and banked with bushes, can also be explored. At any time of year a slow walking tour of Barnston will bring you close to the countryside — the lush meadows spotted with black and white Frisian cows, sheep, horses, pigs, chickens and the simple barnyard things you thought you had forgotten: the strut of a cockerel, the territorial barking of farm dogs, a cat asleep on a fence, the swoop of swallows, even the smell of manure.

The island, being flat and open and threaded through with drainage canals, has somewhat the same flavor as Holland, only less orderly and with a view of mountains. And the river, which has a life of its own, imposes a wilder cast with the noise of passing tugs, log booms moored along the shore, fishboats, gulls and herons and waterbirds. You can look for birds' nests in the hedges, fish off the sandbars at the island's eastern tip, or watch a hawk soaring silently across the fields. (There are red tails and marsh hawks here.) Barnston's population, apart from a couple of separate farms, clusters along the southeastern shore. Many are fishermen; steps lead down from their gardens to wharves where boats are moored and fishnets spread out to dry. The whole island is peaceful and pleasant and you can walk all round in about three hours, passing abandoned homesteads and picturesque barns. Plan to spend the morning here, or bring a picnic and stay all day.

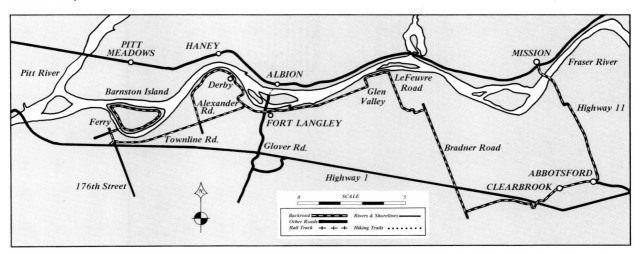

To continue with the tour, cross back to the mainland and retrace your way towards the freeway. Turn left before the freeway bridge onto Townline Road (which turns into Wilson Road) and follow this eastwards to Fort Langley. The road is narrow and undulating and the seven miles is pleasantly covered. The town of Fort Langley, which still keeps some semblance of its pioneer heritage, is a good place to stop for lunch. The fort itself, a national park, is a restoration of the old Hudson's Bay Co. fur-trading post which dates from 1839. The stores, the workshops and the big house have all been furnished with period artifacts, the stockade has been rebuilt and the lookout towers still have their gun slots and cannon. From the lawns overlooking the river you see a view not too changed in 100 years and you begin to understand the feeling of isolation that the HBC men must have had, here in the middle of the wilderness.

If you're a history buff, take a short detour to the original site of Fort Langley, built in 1827 a few miles downriver. Nearby is the locality of the short-lived town of Derby, surveyed by the Royal Engineers as the future capital of the new Crown Colony. Speculators bought lots at outlandish prices. A church and parsonage were built. But before any other construction began, it was decided for defence reasons to move the capital downriver to what is now New Westminster. Derby was abandoned, the church was moved to Maple Ridge, where it still stands, and many Victorian entrepreneurs lost their shirts. To reach the site, return along Wilson Road for about two miles, turn right on Alexander and follow it around the curve of the Fraser. A government cairn marks the site of Old Fort Langley and on the flats nearby was — or was going to be — Derby, the capital city of B.C.

Return again to Fort Langley, but instead of going into the fort take River Road that cuts below it, near the river. As its name suggests, this follows the Fraser, though the railway which runs alongside for a while obscures much of the river view. The twin peaks of Golden Ears are prominent to the north, particularly in winter, and to the south stretch rich water meadows. After 4.8 miles, Glen Valley, one of the little settlements once served by the river steamers, comes into view. Turn left at the general store and follow along beside the river for another 1½ miles, then turn south on Le Feuvre Road. This cuts straight through the valley until it reaches the hills, climbs circuitously up, changing names as it goes, then emerges as McTavish Road to meet Bradner Road. Turn right (south) on Bradner for the village centre and the daffodil fields.

The Bradner area on its high, forested plateau was far from river access and was settled only in 1895. The first farmer was Thomas Bradner. Later, another farmer, Fenwick Fatkin, discovered that the soil and climate here were very good for flowers. He started a bulb farm; others followed and today, at the peak of the season (usually mid-April) you can see fields and fields of daffodils in bloom. Fifty dozen cut blooms are shipped daily from the area to Vancouver and markets across

*The Lower Fraser Valley; old
barns and homesteads,
daffodil fields in April,
a curious ferry to Barnston
Island and always the
mountains on the horizon.*

Canada. At nearly every corner along Bradner and adjoining roads there are stands where you can buy daffodils by the bunch, often for as low as 20¢.

While most of the growers are in the cut flower business and produce only the most popular varieties, others grow and sell the bulbs of exotic species for home gardeners. A good place to see some of these is the Bradner Spring Flower Show, held at the Community Hall around Easter. Here you will find 300 different species of daffodils on display, plus many other spring flowers. If you like what you see, you can order from a grower, and the bulbs will be delivered in time for fall planting.

To return home, follow Bradner Road south, ducking under the freeway, until you come to the old Fraser Highway. Here, you can turn right and follow the highway back to Vancouver via Patullo Bridge and New Westminster, or turn left and go east to Abbotsford and beyond to the No.11 Highway. This crosses over to the north side of the Fraser at Mission where you can pick up Highway No.7 for the return journey to Vancouver. This will take you through Maple Ridge where, if there is time, you can see the old Derby church.

TOUR 4

Ryder Lake Solitudes

To some men's eyes, the area that calls itself Ryder Lake (after a little puddle of a forest-rimmed lake) is nothing special at all: an interlacing of narrow roads, mostly unpaved, some farmhouses, a few rather unkempt fields and a lot of cows. But visit it on a clear day and this hanging valley, poised on benchland between the Fraser Valley and Chilliwack River, becomes a place of astounding mountain views. For the green cow pastures are close, very close, to some of the North Cascade's most spectacular peaks, the jagged sawtooth of Slesse, the abrupt tent shape of Tomahoy, the massive shoulder of Cheam. These mountains, particularly in their white winter dress, dominate the scene. You can't help but lift your eyes.

Just 50 miles from Vancouver and reached quickly by the Highway 1 freeway, Ryder Lake is a good destination for a day's drive, with the possibility of brisk rambles along twisting country lanes that remind one of Europe. Winter is a good time to make the trip, providing the weather is clear and bright and the roads not treacherous. You'll notice the different textures of the furrowed and frosty earth; longer shadows throw barns and farmhouses into sharply etched relief and leafless trees permit views of things hidden by summer's luxuriance.

Drive out on Highway No. 1 east from Vancouver and take the Prest Road exit, just after the Sardis-Cultus Lake turnoff. This road cuts south as straight as an arrow through farmland towards the foothills. Just before it reaches the hills, Bailey Road intersects. Follow the signpost left to Ryder Lake. The road joins onto Elk View Road, climbing in a series of gentle switchbacks, each turn revealing a larger view of the valley below and the checkerboard of Chilliwack city streets, until finally you catch a glimpse of the grey serpentine gleam of the Fraser River itself. There must have been elk up here once, before the loggers and the farmers who followed them robbed the area of its solitude. Today, the elk are gone, but you might see deer in the woods.

The roads at the top of the hill are narrow and winding. Seen on a map they look ridiculously contorted compared to the straight lines in the valley below. And this is the charm of the place. It's different, a little slower, a little quieter, even a little prettier. The lanes — one hesitates to call these meanders "roads" — describe several circles among the fields and woods so that the area is splendid for walks. For instance you could park at the first intersection (Elk View Road and Ryder Lake Road West) and follow Elk View for about 1½ miles, then turn along Ryder Lake downhill (past the lake itself in a sheltering fringe of trees), turn right at the intersection of No. 3 Road, then right again and back to your car. Total distance, less than five miles. There's also a smaller loop, taking in Elk View, No. 3 and Ryder Lake Roads, or a longer one, encompassing them all. Look at the map and you will find other loops, all of them worth the walking.

Scenically, there can be few places in B.C. that so nearly resemble Switzerland, though the fields are rougher, only fairly recently cleared of timber and often, abandoned for farming, beginning

The benchland meadows of Ryder Lake are shaggily beautiful, intersected by little staggering lanes and dominated by spectacular mountain vistas.

The Slesse massif rises in craggy splendor above the fields, is best seen from the end of Elk Lake Road.

to be reclaimed by scrub alder and big-leaf maple. Some of the pastures have never really been cleared. Old stumps remain like bones among the grass. Here and there are old log barns, a school-house, a string of houses, all dwarfed by the magnificent mountains. The best viewpoint for Mount Slesse is at the end of Elk View Road just before the turning to the forestry lookout on Elk Mountain. Turn right on Miller Road, a dead end, and Slesse lies straight ahead across the fields.

On your way home you can take a different route back to the Fraser Valley. Follow No. 3 and Exstrom Roads to Promontory Road which, true to its name, follows the edge of the escarpment with most pleasing views of the valley. This leads you to the Vedder Road just south of Sardis, with the freeway just minutes away to the north. Try this trip in spring, when the dells are thick with dandelions and dogwood blossoms, in the heat of a drowsy clover summer or in the richness of fall. Whatever the season, Ryder Lake has charms.

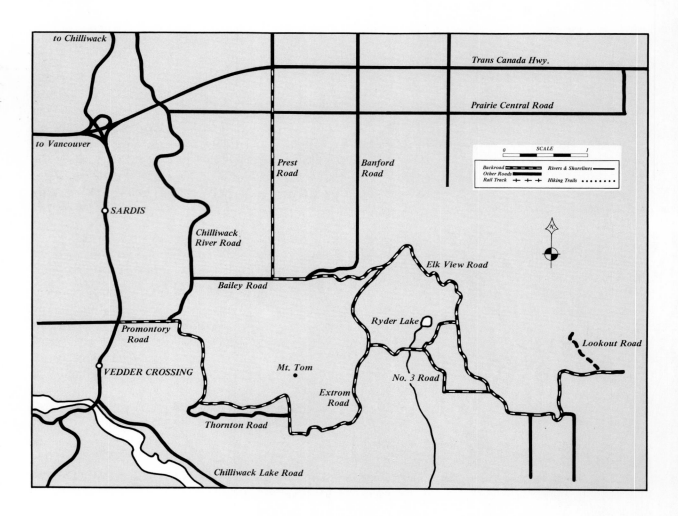

TOUR 5

Lillooet Shortcut

The very first trail to the goldfields of the Cariboo was slashed in 1858 from the Lower Fraser to Lillooet by a route far different from that followed today. The miners came from Fort Victoria across the Strait of Georgia, up the Fraser River and Harrison Lake to Port Douglas, where the Douglas Trail began, built by the miners themselves, under the leadership of the Royal Engineers. It was, in fact, really a series of roads linking up a chain of lakes, 38 miles through the bush to Lillooet Lake and the steamer Marzelle, then 30 miles to Anderson Lake and the sternwheeler Lady of the Lake. From the head of Anderson Lake, a short mile and a half stretch of railway (the first in B.C.) led to Seton Lake and another steamer Champion to the final three-mile trek to Lillooet, where the Cariboo Trail was marked "Mile O". It was only a matter of years before this complex and expensive water route was abandoned in favor of a road up the Fraser Canyon, the route followed by today's Trans-Canada Highway. The earlier route, the first serious, organized attempt at road building in the province, has been forgotten.

There is, however, a relatively new road route from the coast to Lillooet, and this follows eight miles of the original Gold Rush trail between Lillooet and Seton Lakes, then takes an ancient Indian route through the mountains, leaving the precipitously-edged lake route for the hardier trackage of the B.C. Railway. This new route which begins at Mount Currie, four miles east of Pemberton, goes 60 miles on a logging road via Duffey Lake and Cayoosh Creek, bringing Lillooet and the Cariboo beyond some 150 miles closer to Vancouver than by the Fraser Canyon road. An obvious candidate for a highway at some future time, it is, until then, a leisurely backroad, more than making up in time what it saves in distance. Go this way not if you want a speed route to the Cariboo but if you savor old barns, quiet lakes, forests and canyons and mountain views.

The scenic highway along Howe Sound and on to the Whistler ski area is well known to tourists. Few people continue further to the logging town of Pemberton, and fewer still to the Indian settlement of Mount Currie except at rodeo time in May. The village, named for the mountain that overlooks it, contains some excellent examples of square-cut log houses. Sometimes a craft shop is open where you may be lucky enough to find one of the traditional Salish baskets, woven of grass and roots. The women of Mount Currie have not forgotten their Indian skills.

Turn right beside the church along the road that runs into the valley between the Birkenhead and Lillooet Rivers. Some farms here seem deserted, with everything gone to seed. Barn roofs are open fretwork against the sky and thistles invade the orchards. The sandbars along the Birkenhead river may tempt anglers to loiter; at the right time of year the river yields everything from Dolly Varden, to chinooks, cohoes, rainbows and steelhead. It would be difficult to find more idyllic surroundings for a spot of fishing, encircled by the high blue of the mountains.

The eight miles from Mount Currie to Lillooet Lake follow the route of the first Gold Rush

Opposite page: Deserted homestead in the Lillooet River Valley near Mount Currie, the barn roof in ruins and thistles invading the orchard. Right: The web-footed sun sets over Seton Lake. Below: the ice-fields of Mount Matier and Joffre Peak, a glimpse of eternal white above the forest green. Above: Log Indian church near Lillooet.

trail, although the miners travelled it in the opposite direction. There is nothing today to mark the trail's history. But it was here that the famous Cariboo camels, brought in by boat from San Francisco via Victoria in 1862, paced their first trial run on the Cariboo trail. The New Westminster *Columbian,* on May 17, reported that "camels are employed in packing over the Pemberton Portage". The 21 Bactrian camels eventually reached Lillooet where the report was favorable: "They beat any transit we have, either ox, mule or cayuse ponies." Though they could carry monstrous loads and needed little feed, the camels were disastrous additions to the Cariboo freighters. Their strange odor caused the horses of the other packtrains to stampede and the sharp granite of the trail cut their softly padded feet to shreds. A year later, the camels were exiled into the bush, to fend for themselves.

A bridge crosses the Birkenhead River at the head of Lillooet Lake beside the abandoned trestle of an earlier crossing which is taken over in summer by a colony of swallows. The lakehead is a fine spot for spring chinooks. Thirty miles down the lake, reached by government forestry road, lies the mouldering townsite of Port Douglas, once the freight headquarters for the Gold Rush, with stores and restaurants, hotels and saloons, a church and a little log jail that witnessed B.C.'s first legal hanging. There's nothing left today of those rowdy days, merely a clearing in the bush and the ruins of an old logging hostel.

The Duffey Lake Road turns left just past the river bridge and climbs steeply up the mountainside. This road is a private logging road of the Evans Company and you are cautioned to watch out for logging trucks. At the Lillooet end, you are also warned that the road is not suitable for trailers. Like most new logging roads, it's raw, with freshly cut stumps and slash on either side and markers counting down the miles. But though the road is roughly surfaced and traverses several one-way bridges there are no sections that cannot be driven safely by a normal family sedan. The coastal forest through which the road climbs is green and cool and close, starred with dogwood and salmonberry blossoms and wild spirea in spring. Three miles up, the forest parts to reveal a tantalizing glimpse of glaciated peaks, 9,000-foot Mount Matier and Joffre Peak.

Soon the road is at the 4,200-foot divide, the watershed between Coast and Interior, then it winds down into a flat area of burned-over forest, marshy and green and a jungle in summer with flowering fireweed. Against the stark, dead trees and charred stumps the delicate pink of the flowers creates a wistful contrast. The road follows Cayoosh Creek 40 miles all the way to Lillooet, first on the east side, then on the west. The creek was given its name back in Gold Rush days when a pony (cayuse) was found drowned here. Lillooet itself was originally called Cayoosh Flats; its Indian name, which means either "End of the Trail" or "Wild Onion", was bestowed later.

Five miles or so beyond the flats area the road divides, the right branch marked "Duffey Lake Main" heads into logging country on Casper Mountain. Take the left fork which crosses the first of several roaring streams on narrow log bridges. Below on the left through a fringe of trees is the first glimmer of Duffey Lake at 3,700 feet. A second left turn farther on leads to the lakeshore about 20 miles from Lillooet Lake turnoff. There's a campsite here, a sure sign that the lake provides good fishing (rainbows to 12 inches). The lake is five miles long but only half a mile wide, and it fills the valley floor. The creek that drains its northern end is wide and clear and swift-flowing, gathering strength between the mountains. Twenty miles beyond the lake, the canyon deepens; the creek hisses and boils 500 feet below the road at the foot of multi-colored cliffs. Farther along, the road crosses the canyon by a good bridge, and this is an excellent spot to admire the rushing waters below.

Soon however, the canyon views are left behind as the road climbs higher onto a forested bluff, a dry-belt forest of widely-spaced Ponderosa pines and clumps of sage with an astounding view down to Seton Lake far below. Summer sunsets from this vantage point are splendid. Ignore the Texas Creek road which comes in from the right and follow the main road's hairpin bends down to the dam at the lake's end where you will strike pavement again, 57 miles from Mount Currie. As you head into Lillooet notice the little Indian church to your right. Its plank cover has fallen away on one side and you can see massive square cut logs beneath. There is no bell in its decorative

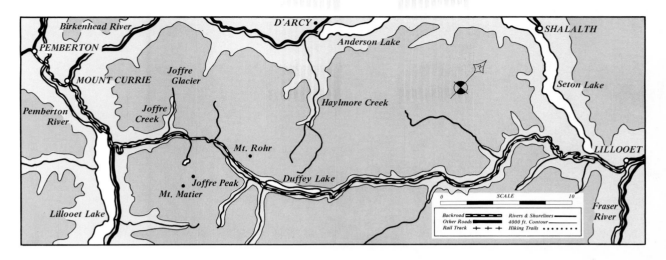

belfry but in the summer of 1975, the church was being given a new roof.

The largest single collection of Indian rock paintings discovered in B.C. lies across the river on rock bluffs above the tracks of the B.C. Railway. To visit them you'll need a good hour; the trip entails a hike along the railway and some rough scrambling. Turn left just after the road crosses the river and drive into the Evans Logging Company yard, less than a mile beyond the church. Stop at the office to ask permission to explore. You will have to sign a waiver of responsibility and wear hard hats through the log unloading yards. Drive through the yard until you can go no further. Scramble up the bank to the railway and walk left along the tracks for a good five minutes, around the curve of the mountain. Below, you will see the confluence of the two rivers, Seton and Cayoosh, and the white road bridge. On the steep rock slope to your right you should be able to pick out a narrow footpath. This will lead up to a huge overhanging rock face, where, faded now after years of weathering, more than a hundred pictographs, ancient Indian figures are painted on the rock.

According to John Corner's book *Pictographs in the Interior of B.C.* several figures are worthy of note. These include a canoe, animals killed with spears and arrows, an eagle holding an animal in its talons and some curious pinwheel designs. You may not be able to find them all but just standing here under this sheltering rock where the Indians must have watched in amazement as the first trickle of gold seekers came down the river, gives a great and satisfying sense of history.

A word of warning. This pictograph site, like others in the province, is protected under the Archeological and Historical Sites Protection Act. Leave it intact, for others to enjoy.

TOUR 6

The Country Lanes of Saanich

Vancouver Island's Saanich Peninsula, one of the province's prettier and gentler places, tends to be forgotten by backroad explorers, perhaps because it is too close to Victoria or because many people drive through it on their way from the ferry terminus at Swartz Bay and feel that they have seen it all already. But there's more to the Peninsula than the 20-minute highway drive can show. It's a small, very English part of B.C., at least in looks. There is nothing dramatic about the place, no great mountains or rushing rivers, just little fields and farms and copses where the pleasures of country life can be appreciated. It's best perhaps in spring, adazzle with wild easter lilies and shooting stars, gardens stuffed with daffodils and tulips and every imaginable kind of flowering shrubs and trees. But ripe summer and fall have their own special appeal too, and at any season you'll likely hear the heart-soaring song of the English skylark.

In the early 1900s, homesick English settlers brought over a hundred pairs of these larks for release near Victoria. The birds liked the fields of Saanich and settled down happily to sing and soar and breed. By 1962 their numbers had increased tenfold but lately, creeping urbanization has destroyed some of the rough pastures where the larks nest, and the population has dwindled. At last count, only about 40 pairs were seen. You can still find English skylarks in Saanich, but they become increasingly rare and the pilgrimages of bird lovers from all over North America has taken on a new sense of urgency. One day, the larks may all be gone.

The Saanich Peninsula was one of the earliest areas in B.C. to be settled. Victoria the Fort was surveyed in 1842, the Colony of Vancouver Island founded seven years later and it wasn't long before settlers were spreading out into the thick woods of Saanich to carve themselves homesteads. The first farmers were the Thomsons who cleared land on the slopes of Mount Newton in 1858 and later gave land for St. Stephen's Church, the first in the area and one of the oldest in the province. As population grew, the trails linking the farms and settlements became wagon roads. The Victoria Stage made daily journeys from the city to North Saanich, leaving the stables at 8 a.m. via West Saanich Road and returning by East Saanich Road at 6 p.m., a long day's journey. In 1893, Victoria businessman Robert Irving and North Saanich pioneers Henry and Julius Brethour started to build the Victoria and Sidney Railway to provide improved transportation for Saanich residents, a link with steamships to the mainland, and an opportunity for Victoria residents to get cheap firewood. From the Hillside Street station, trains ran twice a day, leaving at 7 a.m. and 4 p.m., returning from Sidney at 9 and 5.30. The trip took 50 minutes and cost 50 cents. For nearly 20 years, the V & S Railway had the peninsula to itself. Then the B.C. Electric Railway built a competitive line, and this was soon followed by the Canadian National. The Saanich Peninsula — all 20 miles of it — was served by three railways. Today there are none.

Modern routes through the peninsula, dominated by Highway 17 to Swartz Bay, are mainly

Saanich in springtime:
An outburst of erythroniums
in a woodland glade, pink
shooting stars and
clam-diggers on
Patricia Bay mudflats.

the old stage coach roads, now paved but still for the most part narrow and sinuous and hemmed in with little hedges. You won't want to travel much faster than the stage coaches, either, for a day is hardly long enough to dally in all the places along the way. There are beaches for clam-digging and bird watching, countless little lanes to meander down, old churches, old inns, farmhouses selling all kinds of country fresh produce. Dairy farming and soft fruits, particularly loganberries, are the major commercial interests but flowers are also important. In April, fields and fields of daffodils are in bloom. The area also fosters an industry unique in Canada — the growing of Christmas holly.

Visitors from the Mainland can start their explorations almost immediately they clear the Swartz Bay ferry dock. At the top of the hill, turn sharp right onto Landsend Road which circuits the north end of the peninsula around Beacon Point. Thick woods obscure the ocean view, but it's a pleasant, quiet road. Round the corner of Cloake Hill the road joins West Saanich Road for the meandering southward journey towards Victoria, joining the highway at Royal Oak some 15 miles down. Lacing between these main roads is a network of crossroads, each one worthy of travel. You can explore them all, if you have the time. Here are some of the interesting places around the peninsula circuit, in roughly counter-clockwise order from Landsend Road:

The sandy sweep of Patricia Bay is a good spot at low tide for feast quantities of little neck and butter clams. Watch for small depressions in the sand or for a tell-tale squirt of water, then dig down about a foot on the seaward side. On weekends there will be many seafood lovers on the hunt, but weekdays you might just have the beach to yourselves. The bay is also good for shorebirds, particularly in winter. The houses along the road here are a delight, some quaintly gabled and named in the English fashion "Seawatch" or "Snughaven", their gardens bright with flowers. Just look at those roses! Stop at the little brown church at the corner of Mills Road. Built in 1885, Holy Trinity has a neat graveyard and in spring real English wood violets, the fragrant ones, grow in the ditch. Beyond the church, the open fields of Victoria Airport provide territory for day-hunting short-eared owls and nesting sites for skylarks. McTavish Road, beyond the airport, links up with Highway 17 and Bazan Bay. Mount Newton Cross Road, further south, is perhaps a more interesting road for it ambles east to the old village of Saanichton on East Saanich Road. A farm near the turnoff sells leeks and Jerusalem artichokes and there are Highland cattle in the field. Two miles along, a shaggy, sloping field near the school is a good place for skylarks. Stand quietly beside the hedge and listen. The lark's song, uttered only when the bird is ascending into the sky, is unmistakable, a tireless torrent of melody. The bird itself, streaky brown and little bigger than a sparrow, is often difficult to see, a mere twinkling speck against the sky.

Further south down West Saanich Road, past Our Lady of the Assumption Church, a right turn leads to Brentwood Bay and the ferry across Saanich Inlet to Mill Bay, a 20-minute trip that enables you to bypass Victoria if you are heading up the Island. And nearby there's a campground and boat launching ramp run by the Tsartlip Indian band. Butchart's Gardens are at the end of a beautiful winding road planted with flowering cherry trees and blossoming verges. A popular tourist spot, the gardens' 25 acres of flowering loveliness are always worth a visit. Just beyond the Butchart turning, the Cock Pheasant sits in its own little flower garden. A pretty cottage hung with flowering vines and bird feeders, the Cock Pheasant reminds one of an English country inn, with its colorful roadside sign. Here you can have lunch, dinner or afternoon tea, simple country-fresh foods, well cooked and served with a friendly flair. Further along, Prospect Lake General Store has a wide wooden verandah and an old-fashioned ambience. Step inside and buy the kids an ice cream.

The Dominion Astrophysical Observatory, east up a steeply winding road, is open on weekdays from 9.15 to 4.30 from April to October. The grounds alone are well worth a visit. High on a rocky outcrop, the observatory domes seem something from science fiction among the gnarled Gary oaks, thick moss and wildflowers, with far off, the shimmer of snow on the Olympic Mountains across the strait. The 72-inch telescope is not primarily for optical study, so there is little for the layman to see. Light collected from outer space is fed directly into machines for study and analysis by scientists. On Saturday nights however (from 8 to 10, April through November), visitors can watch the observatory in action. The roof slides back, the giant telescope swings around to focus on a particular star and you can stay long enough to understand some of the work of the astronomers. Dress warmly. No heating is permitted inside the observatory.

Unless you want to go on to Victoria, you must turn off West Saanich Road before it merges with the highway. The first left turn south of the observatory takes you onto the Old West Road which snakes behind the observatory hill to join Oldfield and Keating Cross Road and then onto East Saanich Road which leads north to Saanichton. At the intersection of this road with Newton Cross Road is the two-storeyed, balconied Prairie Inn (now a store), built in 1893 to replace the earlier Prairie Tavern established in 1858 by a former Hudson's Bay Co. baker, Henry Simpson. Nearby is St. Stephen's Church, built in 1862, one of the oldest in B.C. Saanichton, centre of the soft fruit and flower growing area — 13 million daffodils a year are shipped from here — is the home of B.C.'s oldest agricultural fair, the oldest in fact west of the Great Lakes. Founded in 1871, it is still held every September. On the fairgrounds are two museums — the Pioneer Museum housed in a log cabin and the Centennial Museum which displays old farm machinery and household artifacts. Saanichton is also the site of some of the newest agricultural research. The federal government's research and plant quarantine station is further north along East Saanich Road near McTavish. Visitors are welcome in the greenhouses which specialize in the propagation of ornamental shrubs, vegetables and flowers.

Sidney on the eastern side of Pat Bay Highway is a town worth a visit if only for the stupendous view of Mount Baker floating above the boats in the harbor. And from the ferry slip nearby you can contemplate the possibilities of taking a cruise through the San Juan Islands. It's a good spot to end the day.

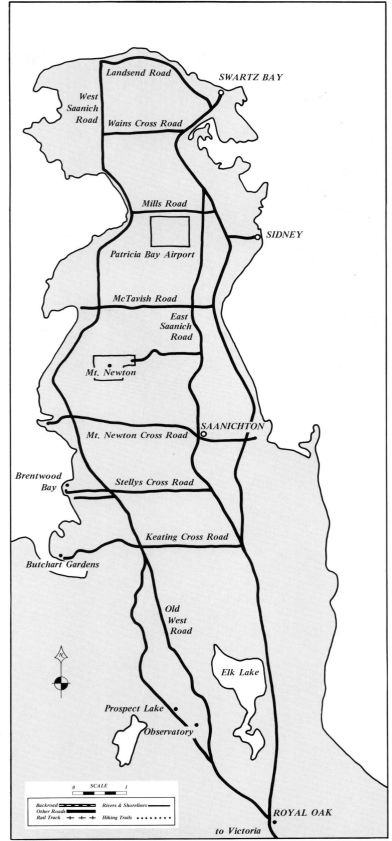

The West Coast Road

One of British Columbia's oldest roads must be the route from Victoria to Metchosin and Sooke, which rambles around the southernmost tip of Vancouver Island. Built in 1852, only nine years after the founding of Fort Victoria, the trail provided a link with the newly-established farms and settlements that grew up along the coast. It was a rough trail at first, a constant aggravation to the settlers who had been promised something better. By the time it was good enough for stage coaches, homesteaders further north, from Jordan River to Port Renfrew, were clamoring for a road, but this, the West Coast Road, was not fully completed until 1957.

The West Coast Road to Port Renfrew and the return loop through the forests to Shawnigan Lake makes a good day's excursion from Victoria. If you have a historical turn of mind there is much of interest: old coaching inns, forts, lighthouses, churches and monuments. The scenery is splendid — beaches and rocky headlands, neat fields and wilderness forest, with the mountains of Washington's Olympic Peninsula high and hazy across the strait. Along the way there is so much to do that you will want to return often, as many Victorians already do.

From Victoria look for Highway 14, which branches off Highway 1 near the head of Esquimalt

Inlet. At the inlet bridge, Six-Mile House, opened in 1855 as Parson's Bridge Hotel, was the first of several refreshment houses along the stage coach route. The inn is closed now, but stop on the bridge anyway and look south to see the brick ruins of the naval arsenal on Cole Island. Less than a mile further, branch left and follow the signs 1½ miles to Fort Rodd Hill, built in 1895 to defend the British Royal Navy base in Esquimalt Harbor. Now a National Historic Park, it scatters its stalwart brick buildings over 40 acres of rocky parkland bright in spring with dog-tooth violets, blue camas and the pink clusters of shooting stars. Deer roam the woodlands and the shore is an excellent place for birdwatching (black oystercatchers can be seen here). Fisgard Lighthouse, connected to the fort grounds by a rock causeway, has been on guard here since 1860, a dramatic white tower and a square building of warm red brick that before the days of automation, used to house the keeper of the light. It is planned to restore and furnish the keeper's residence to its 1860 condition, but until then the lighthouse buildings are closed to the public.

From the fort, double back a way and take Ocean Boulevard down to Esquimalt Lagoon, a federal bird sanctuary where black brant geese and other birds gather in great numbers during the fall migration. The road crosses a humped-back wooden bridge and onto a spit of land between the lagoon and the sea — a great spot for a picnic. Continue along the spit and up Lagoon Road to the Metchosin Road, on an alternate loop to Highway 14. The settlement of Metchosin (the word is Indian for "stinking fish") lies five miles from the lagoon. Just before the general store at the intersection of Happy Valley Road, stop for a moment at the little Anglican church of St. Mary the Virgin, which dates from 1873. Its tangled graveyard under mossy Gary oaks is gay in July with wild marguerites which sprawl over the marble headstones of the pioneers.

If it is time for tea (this corner of B.C. still preserves that honorable British custom), drive along the Weir's Beach road to Fernie Farm, where afternoon teas — homemade scones and clotted Devonshire Cream — are served daily from 3 to 5 p.m. Return to Metchosin and take Happy Valley Road back to Highway 14. The schoolhouse, a little way along, dates from 1872. Turn left on Highway 14 for the West Coast Road and the Royal Ensign Hotel, founded in 1894 by Edward Cutler as a stage coach saloon, and known then as 17-Mile House. Unlike Six-Mile, this old inn is still open for business.

The first glimpse of Sooke Harbour, a deeply indented basin almost cut off by fingers of land, is an industrial one — the log booms and timber yards of B.C. Forest Products — but these are soon passed and you're at Milne's Landing, named for Edward Milne who opened a store here in 1893 and built a wharf so that he could bring in his goods by sea. The old Milne homestead (built by Edward's grandfather in 1888) still stands on the northeast side of the bridge over the Sooke River.

Ten miles upstream, the Leech River was the scene of Vancouver Island's first and only gold rush. A government expedition led by Dr. Robert Brown discovered gold on the Leech in July, 1864 and soon hundreds of men were on the river with pick and goldpan. The settlement of Leechtown mushroomed overnight where the Leech ran into the Sooke; a mule trail was put through to the diggings and C.A. Bayley ran daily pack trains from Sooke. By spring of next year, $100,000 had been recovered. By fall, the gold and the miners had gone and deserted Leechtown was left moldering in the forest. Today, only the ruins of the gold commissioner's log cabin can be found, and a government cairn has been erected to mark the spot. The Sooke River Road leads four miles up the east side of the river to Sooke River Potholes Park, where the softer rock of the river bed has been eroded by boulders into natural swimming holes, a welcome spot on a hot afternoon. On the opposite side of the river bridge, the Castle Hotel, its turrets and battlements festooned with ivy, feeds hungry travellers (yes, afternoon tea is served).

In 1789, the Spaniard Manuel Quimper, sent to explore the Strait of Juan de Fuca, landed in Sooke Inlet and took possession of the land in the name of the king of Spain, naming the bay Porto de Nevillo Cigado. Spain withdrew her claim to the coast six years afterwards and the area was surveyed by the British who gave British names to everything in sight, except for Sooke itself, which already had an Indian name. The village is a centre for commercial fishing and lumbering. Its oysters

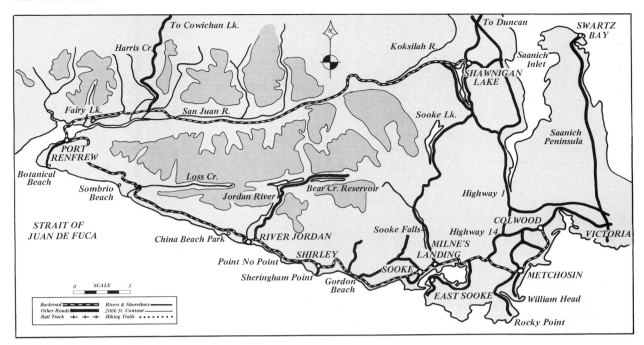

are famous; you can find oyster beds at a couple of places along the bay. It is also an excellent place for sports fishing. Resorts here supply boats, tackle, bait and guides for excursions into the strait.

At Maple Avenue, which leads down to the government wharf, a cairn commemorates the landing of the first settler, Walter Grant, who established a 100-acre homestead here in August 1849, bringing with him from Scotland eight other workers. He stayed only a short time, selling his land in 1853 to John Muir, but he left a legacy that no one can ignore. He made a trip to Hawaii, where the British consul gave him some seeds of the English broom. He planted these seeds in Sooke on his return and since then, English broom has spread its gold over the whole of southern Vancouver Island. The hill above the harbor is called Broom Hill, in memory of Grant's gift while Mount Manuel Quimper, higher and further to the east, surveys all of the basin which its namesake once claimed.

Just beyond the village, turn left along Whiffin Spit Road for the mile drive to the shore and this remarkable strip of land that almost seals off the inlet from the sea. Here you can dig for clams, fish for cutthroat trout, picnic on the beach or stop at Sooke Harbour House on the shore for tea or the night.

Beyond Whiffin Spit, the views of the ocean are obscured by a fringe of forest almost all the way to Jordan River, except for Gordon Beach, the first real West Coast beach along the road, where summer cabins on the oceanside hide the view. At the community of Shirley, founded 1885, turn left at the red community hall for Sheringham Point Lighthouse, open to the public on weekdays for guided tours from 2 to 3 p.m. If the lighthouse is closed, park near the entrance and walk down the trail beside the wire fence onto the headland for a fine view of the lighthouse, built in 1912, and some lovely picnic spots on the cliffs. Another scenic lookout is at Point No Point, 3½ miles further on, where a lodge provides accommodation, meals and afternoon teas from 2 to 5 p.m. A good trail here leads to the beach. The point acquired its odd name because from one survey station it showed as a prominent headland, while from another, no point of land was seen at all. The official survey in 1895 called it Glacier Point, but local residents had the name changed back to the earlier one in 1957.

River Jordan, about halfway between Victoria and Port Renfrew, was named by the Spaniards for Alejandro Jordan, the chaplain to Lt. Francisco Eliza who visited the area in 1790. In its early years, it was a logging community; now the River Jordan provides hydro power for most of southern Vancouver Island from a plant built in 1911 and expanded 40 years later. There's a log bridge over the river and you will probably see some of the great West Coast breakers rolling in along the shore. The beach is a favorite with surfers. Rayonier of Canada has provided a picnic area at the bridge and you can fish here for ocean perch. There is a hotel, a restaurant and a gas station which also sells fresh crabs.

While the route from River Jordan to Port Renfrew, another 36 miles, is a public road, logging trucks use it too. The first nine miles are paved, but beyond it's rough gravel, badly washboarded on the hills and in places narrow and winding. But it gives access to three excellent West Coast beaches. The first, China Beach, a provincial park, is 2½ miles beyond Jordan River. A 15-minute downhill hike from the parking lot leads through a really beautiful stretch of old open forest to a wide sandy beach. Ten miles along, the road bridges Loss Creek where there is a small shady park for picnics and a trail leading downstream for fishing. Three miles further, at the top of a rough, winding hill, a roadside parking lot marks the start of a 30-minute trail to Sombrio Beach with its cave and waterfall and sandstone shelf pitted with tide pools, an excellent place for marine exploration. Indians believed Sombrio to be the warmest place on the island and came here for cures. The water, however, is cold.

Just before Port Renfrew, the road branches right to the lumber company town and roads leading to Shawnigan and Cowichan Lakes. Turn left here for a visit to the long government wharf (it's old and decrepit), the hotel and store. Left again before the wharf, another road leads down to Botanical Beach, a spectacular area of sandstone ledges, worn by the sea into pools which at low tide trap many kinds of marine creatures. In the tidepools, reefs and kelp-covered rocks a rich variety of sea life can be observed. Around the turn of the century, Minnesota University established a marine research station here, and built log lodges and laboratories. But the station was abandoned after 10 years and none of the buildings remain. In the Second World War the Royal Engineers came to Port Renfrew to repair the plank logging road and continue it to Botanical Beach where they built a gun emplacement which fortunately never saw use.

The San Juan River which enters the sea at Port Renfrew was well known to early Spanish explorers. Quimper in 1740 called the harbor Puerto de San Juan, harbored ships at the river mouth and ran a mule train up to the headwaters where the sailors searched for gold. They had mines at several places. In 1859, Hugh McKay of Sooke investigated the Spanish diggings along the San Juan and found two other men already working the area. More gold was discovered in the late 1860s and more still in the 1870s but never in sufficient amounts to start a stampede.

The San Juan River valley, though heavily forested, consists of deep black loam suitable for agriculture and early on the government tried to encourage settlement. In 1889, Frank Hobbs obtained 1,000 acres; others followed, homesteading up the river as far as Lost Creek, for the government promised that a road would soon be put through from Victoria. At first, the settlement was called Port San Juan, but because of confusion with the American San Juan Islands, the name was changed to Port Renfrew. By 1900, 100 homesteaders were clearing the valley land. Their only contact with civilization was either by sea, or by way of the Lifesaving Trail, a rough trail hacked out of the bush along the shore beside the telegraph line. This was established primarily to help shipwrecked sailors; the coast was notorious for storms and earned the name Graveyard of the Pacific. Once ashore, the sailors could reach one of the telegraph stations (in shacks along the way) and summon help. The settlers had been promised a real road, and when none materialized, they drifted away, abandoning their hard-won clearings to the forest. The West Coast Road was finally built in 1957, but by then, the riches lay in forestry not agriculture.

Port Renfrew is the company town of British Columbia Forest Products which owns the timber rights in the area; it is also an important fishing port. The area is much appreciated for its excellent sports fishing and wilderness atmosphere. There's a boat launching site just before the long wooden bridge over the San Juan River mouth for fishing in the bay (chinooks in April, halibut in May, giant coho in the fall). There is good smelting off the beach from July until September and trout fishing at the river mouth. The townsite is also the beginning of the Lifesaving Trail, which has been restored

Top: St. Mary's Church, Metchosin.
Right: Dramatic log suspension
bridge on the San Juan Valley Road
to Shawnigan Lake: Above: One of
the rock coves facing the Olympics.

for hikers all the way north to Bamfield. Hikers must be ferried across the Gordon River to the beginning of the trail, now part of the Pacific Rim National Park, and from there it's a rugged week-long hike.

On nearby Fairy Lake, really a swelling of the river channel, the forest company has set up a good campsite, with nature trails, a boat launching site and swimming area. The lake was homesteaded by a Dutchman Vander Wower around the turn of the century. He found the soil well suited for the cultivation of rhubarb. His crop grew so big that he decided to enter some in the World's Fair, held in Chicago, and the rhubarb from Fairy Lake won first prize.

Drive four miles beyond Fairy Lake for the junction with the Harris Creek Road to Cowichan Lake, closed during operating hours. Turn right at the junction and head for Shawnigan Lake along a public road, but once again, beware of logging trucks. This 40-mile-stretch of forest road passes some prime fishing spots along the upper San Juan and Koksilah Rivers, and there are some splendid old bridges to mark the way. Four miles after the turnoff, a wooden suspension bridge, with a span of 264 feet, is known locally as the Black Suspension Bridge. Here, at the forest company picnic and campsite, you can launch a boat to float down the river to Fairy Lake.

The bridge over Bear Creek, some seven miles further on, used to cause difficulties for travellers because road graders could not navigate it and the area beyond was always in bad condition. However the forest company has now built a bypass. When you reach a sign saying "Bear Creek Bridge out" don't turn back in despair, but take the right hand road which climbs up and around the creek. This is the bypass route, which rejoins the road just the other side of the old bridge. Park here and walk back to see the trestle bridge, 254 feet high above the river.

Four miles past Bear Creek the road comes over a hill and descends suddenly to a reverse curve suspension bridge high above a canyon, a surprise if you are not expecting it. The road seems to disappear. Eight miles further on, keep an eye for a clump of trees on the left standing like an island in the midst of logging slash. This clump contains a patch of wild rhododendron which has been spared the logger's axe.

At the road forks three miles further still, the BCFP logging road takes a shortcut, while the public road goes left. The logging road is the better and faster route, but it should be used only in non-operating hours. The two roads converge for the run beside the beautiful Koksilah River, which rushes, clear and lovely, beside the road for about four miles. (Steelhead to 15 lbs. here.) Keep north of Shawnigan Lake for the quickest route to Highway 1 near Mill Bay and the run to Victoria over the Malahat Highway.

TOUR 8

Cowichan Lake Circuit

Anglers will need no introduction to Cowichan Lake. It's Vancouver Island's undisputed year-round champion producer of giant cutthroat and rainbow trout. The Cowichan River which drains the lake into Cowichan Bay, is equally famous for fighting brown trout taken in summer with a dry fly and for 20-lb winter steelhead. Reached from Duncan by an excellent paved road to Lake Cowichan, the community at the lake's end, Cowichan Lake is girdled by a road that makes a grand 50-mile circle tour even if you aren't a fisherman. And down the lake other forestry roads lead further afield to Port Renfrew and Bamfield through the deep forests that cover the interior of Vancouver Island like a cloak — a land of green shadows, jungled with ferns and moss. The country is logging country; giant trucks have right of way and you can see close up the various stages of forestry, from the destruction and chaos of a recently cleared section, to newly planted forests of several different ages, and, occasionally, a glimpse of virgin forest. Forestry companies allow the public to use the roads and have made several attractive little camp and picnic sites along the way.

The Cowichan/Duncan area was first settled in August, 1862 when HMS Hecate landed 100 homesteaders at Cowichan Bay. The town of Duncan, however, did not exist until after the Esquimalt and Nanaimo Railway cut through the area in the 1880s. A group of settlers petitioned the railway for a station on the farm of William Duncan, a central location in the valley. The station was built, and the following year the townsite was laid out, originally as Duncan's Farm, then called Alderley, Duncan's Crossing, Duncan's Station, Duncan's and finally, Duncan. The new highway to Lake Cowichan parallels the Cowichan River and there are access roads at several places. Fish ladders were built at Skutz Falls in 1955 to help migrating salmon upstream and the area is now an excellent spot for family fishing and picnicking, with flat rocky areas that invite the sunbather. Downriver from the falls is a pedestrian suspension bridge giving access to a Fish and Game Association trail on the opposite shore that follows the river all the way from Duncan to Lake Cowichan. The bridge is safe, but scary as it swings high above the river.

The community of Lake Cowichan dates from 1910, though the first road was put through from the coast as early as 1885. The roads beyond are paved to Youbou on the north side of the lake and Honeymoon Bay on the south, but the rest of the lake circuit is rough gravel, hilly in places, with a recommended speed limit of 30 mph. The roads around the lake are open to the public at all times, but beyond, they are working logging roads, open only during non-operating hours. To make the lake circuit, turn left at the Cowichan Bridge and head for Honeymoon Bay. First stop of interest is Mesachie Lake, former site of the Hillcrest Lumber Co. sawmills which closed in 1968. Nearby is a provincial government forestry research station where the public is welcome,

Cowichan Lake woods are lovely, dark and deep, with big bumpy bandages of moss and tall ferns. Boating on the lake from Heather Campsite and strolling through lakeshore meadows are good autumn pursuits. Below left: A backwater slough of the Cowichan River.

and here, too is the forestry road via Nineteen and Harris Creeks to Port Renfrew.

Despite its romantic sounding name, Honeymoon Bay eight miles along the road is not at all a picturesque village but a sawmill settlement of Rayonier Canada Ltd. The view across the lake from here is industrial — log booms in the water and the smoke from the mills hazing the lake in shades of misty blue. Honeymoon Bay was settled in 1886 by Henry March who cleared a farm here. It used to take him three days to get his produce to market at Duncan by raft and ox-team but his farm prospered where others closer to Duncan failed. And the March holding is still the only farm-land on the lake. The name of the bay comes from plans one settler had to fetch a bride from England to his home here. He never returned, but the name was fixed forever. A right turn down to the lake at end of pavement here leads to Gordon Bay provincial campground and boat launching, a popular spot for anglers, and half a mile further there's a wildflower reserve, a few acres of forest set aside by Western Forest Industries complete with rotting stumps and primitive trails. Here, under the ragged banners of Spanish moss you can find flowers typical of the West Coast rainforest. In fall, it's a good spot for mushrooms.

Be sure to call in at B.C. Forest Products' Caycuse campsite, five miles down the road, if only for a short stroll. Here, the forest floor is a luxuriant carpet of sword fern and the trees, mostly big-leaf maples, are gnarled and knobbly with great bumpy bandages of moss. There are about 25 campsites here, some excellent nature trails and a shingle beach for boat launching. At the Caycuse office of BCFP just down the road the recreation officer will be glad to give information on hiking and fishing, and can also organize tours of forestry operations. The company coffee shop, gas station and other services here are also available to the public.

Beyond Caycuse, the road becomes mountainous, twisty and steep so drive with particular care. Another five miles will bring you to the head of the lake at Nitinat where roads lead through the forest wilderness to Nitinat Lake, Bamfield and Port Alberni. To complete the lake circle, keep right at the junction, past B.C. Forest Products' Heather Campsite where there is a good beach for swimming and boat launching. Three miles further, around the north end of the lake, there's a flat meadow promontory that seems to have once been cleared and settled. Shaw Creek swirls through meadows where the grass grows tall and where in summer, wild strawberries lurk. A grown over trail leads into this area just past the Shaw Creek bridge. Both this creek, and McKay Creek four miles along the road provide good trout fishing where they enter the lake. Ten miles further, over Cottonwood and Wardroper Creeks the gravel road turns to pavement and you're at the headquarters of B.C. Forest Products and Youbou, the lumber town beyond. Lake Cowichan, the end of the circuit, lies nine miles ahead.

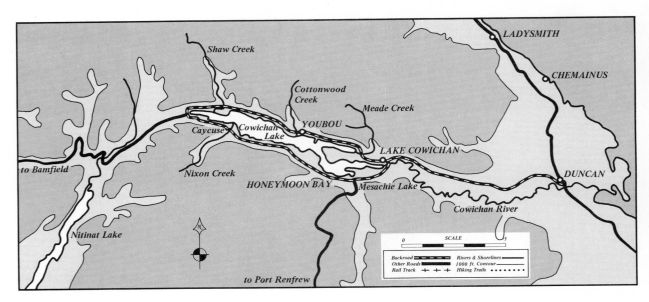

TOUR 9

Tulameen Stage Route to Aspen Grove

The Valley of the Tulameen is largely forgotten now, bypassed many years ago by an easier and faster highway route from Princeton to Merritt. But these 40 miles, once the main stage route from the coast, lead through an area that is not only most scenic, but notable for the scope of its history. Indians came here to trade for precious red ochre; the fur brigades camped by Otter Lake on their way north from Hope to Nicola; gold-mining towns bloomed and faded along the creeks to be followed in turn by equally ephemeral mining camps of coal. The road makes possible a good circle tour from Princeton; the old road joins the highway just south of Aspen Grove. Or you can continue further on backroads over to the ghosts of the Kettle Valley Railway and the Coldwater River all the way to Merritt. This last section will add another 40 miles to your trip.

The route begins at Princeton, the little town at the confluence of the Similkameen and Tulameen Rivers. Renamed after the Prince of Wales in 1860, the settlement once went by the prettier name of Vermilion Forks because of the red or vermilion ochre found on a cliff up the Tulameen. Long before Europeans arrived, the area was an Indian trading centre. Tribes came from as far away as the Great Plains to barter for the red earth, which they used for paint. The Indian word for red earth is "Tulameen" and to them Princeton was "Yak-Tulameen", the Place of the Red Earth. The red bluff, a seam of metamorphosed coal, is still there today rising up from the river about three miles from Princeton. The road climbs above it. To reach the bluff, a good source of petrified wood, agates and fossils, it is best to walk along the railway tracks.

Drive down Princeton's Bridge Street. The old stage coach route swings sharp left over the bridge and climbs steeply to avoid the Tulameen canyon. The road is paved for the first mile or so, but soon narrows to a thin twisting ledge perched precariously on the river bluffs. There are several blind corners here, so you must drive with care. This is the roughest part of the route. Around the bluffs the road widens, running smoothly through forest down to the valley floor and along beside the river to Coalmont, 11 miles from Princeton. Coalmont is almost a ghost town, founded around the turn of the century by the Columbia Coal and Coke Co. which mined the eight-foot seams of valley coal by the room-and-pillar method. In the optimism of the day it was believed that the "Mountain of Coal" would last forever and that the Tulameen would become a prosperous, industrial valley. The Coalmont Courier, founded in 1912, called the town "the City of Destiny, the coal-mining metropolis of Southern B.C." and expected "a population of 10,000 in the near future. And the Kettle Valley Railway built a line up from Princeton to transport the wealth.

Happily, perhaps, for the Tulameen Valley, Coalmont did not live up to expectation. The easily-extracted surface coal was soon exhausted and it proved uneconomical to mine the deeper seams. The mines at Blakeburn above Granite Creek continued to be profitable, however, and Coalmont lingered for a while as the railway shipping centre. But when the Blakeburn mines closed, Coalmont

The Tulameen Valley is a place of memories, of ghost town Granite Creek, sitting derelict in a field of spring buttercups; of historic Thynne Ranch, once a stage coach stop; of unidentified mining ruins slipping quietly into oblivion.

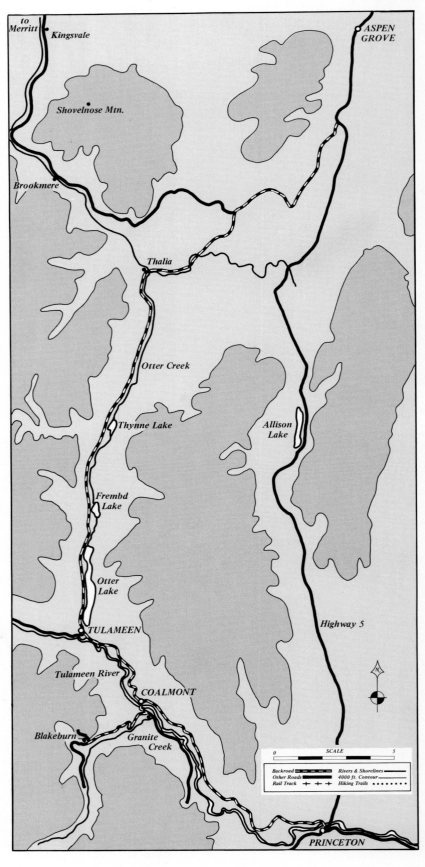

gave up the ghost — but not quite. The big old hotel is still open for business and while the other wooden false-fronted stores are closed (including the meat market, once the liquor store, opposite) a new concrete building, the Coalmont Emporium, has recently opened its doors to serve growing numbers of recreational residents who have settled in the area for fishing, hiking, rock-hounding and exploring. For the Tulameen is a beautiful valley. The mines have not ruined it.

Coalmont was founded on coal. Granite Creek, one of the prettiest ghost towns in the province, grew rich on placer gold. To reach the townsite, go straight along the road beside the Coalmont Hotel (the main road swings right) and cross the river over a little wooden bridge. A mile along the north side of the river, Granite Creek tumbles down from the mountains and beside its gold-laden waters the town of Granite Creek (or Granite City) grew up. Gold was discovered here in 1885 by a cowboy called Johnny Chance who was driving cattle over the Tulameen Trail (the old brigade route) to Hope. News of the strike drew miners like a magnet from the gold camps of the Cariboo and the Kootenays and even from the security of a steady job with the Canadian Pacific Railway. Miners cleared the benchland at the confluence of the streams and their camp soon grew to a lusty settlement of 2,000 with no fewer than 13 saloons, including the famous Cariboo House. There were 10 stores, two blacksmiths, two jewellers and many cabins — well over 200 buildings strung out along the three main streets. Waterwheels lined the banks of the creek, which proved to be extraordinarily rich ($90,000 in gold was taken in the first three months) and, for a placer creek, long lasting. The boom lasted for three glorious years, and then trickled to a stop. The creek and the town were abandoned.

Plentiful while it lasted, the placer gold of Granite Creek was intermixed with another mineral, light in color and equal in weight so that it was difficult to separate them. This "white gold", as the miners called it with curses, was seemingly valueless and it was dumped into the bush. But one Swedish miner named Johanssen was intrigued by the white metal and collected it in a bucket. After a couple of years the bucket, holding a good 20 lbs, was full. When the Swede left the creek, he buried the bucket and its load somewhere near his cabin and like the rest of the miners, he never returned. Years later more sophisticated mining men discovered that the "white gold" was platinum, worth far more than gold. Old Granite Creek claims were feverishly reworked, garbage dumps searched and many of the miners' shacks were burned down so that platinum could be recovered from their ashes. Old-timers also remembered the bucket of platinum that Johanssen had buried, but despite a long search, it was never found. Presumably it is still there somewhere, between the few crumbling relics of the gay old town. (The Tulameen River system is one of only two areas in the world where free platinum is found. The other is the Amur River in Russia.)

While Granite Creek has been deserted for nearly 75 years, enough remains for it to merit the ghost town description. Half a dozen buildings stand in varying degrees of repair. Only one has been identified, the F.P. Cook store, now a roofless log structure. Cook's advertised itself as the oldest established trading post in the Similkameen, and also had branches at Princeton and Coalmont. The river bench is a popular but unofficial place for camping, though bottle diggers and souvenir hunters have made the ground hillocky with their diggings. You can pan for gold in the creek; it's one of the streams that can be counted on to show some color in the pan. Above the creek, a government concrete cairn used to mark the site of the old gold town, but vandals have stolen its bronze plaque — a sad comment on our times.

Six miles further up the Granite Creek road is the coal-mining ghost town of Blakeburn, once connected to Coalmont 1,600 feet below by an aerial tram. The settlement is remembered most for "Black Wednesday" of August 1930 when a terrible explosion at the No. 4 mine killed all but one of the 46 men underground. Blakeburn is also thought of with gratitude because it was the only mine in the area to keep operating through the Depression. It finally closed down for good in 1940 and today only one decaying cabin marks its site.

Retrace your way to Coalmont, turn left at the hotel and drive up the empty main street, following the Tulameen River five miles to the settlement of Tulameen, between the river and Otter

Gaunt ghost of the Dominion Hotel at Tulameen may soon be torn down. Below: Relics of Granite Creek, once the liveliest gold town in the province.

Lake. In stage coach days, Tulameen was called Otter Flats, and long before that, men of the fur brigade, who camped here on their way from Hope to Nicola, knew it as Campement des Femmes. It was here, an ancient campsite, that the women and children would be left when the men went into the mountains. A mining camp grew up here in the Gold Rush days of the 1880s, but it faded when Granite Creek declined. Years later, the town was revived as a coal mining centre, but it faded again when the coal mines closed. Today, while it's a sad relic of its former size and importance — the huge Dominion Hotel is an empty ruin — the town seems to be making a comeback as a summer settlement. Some of the old homes have been refurbished as summer cabins, and new cottages have been built along the west lakeshore. Otter Lake provides good swimming and other water activities.

At Tulameen, the stage coach road that we are following leaves the river and heads north, up the west side of Otter Lake and into the Otter Creek valley. The Kettle Valley Railway also takes this route to Merritt but travels along the east side of the lake. Two provincial park sites are on the lake: one at the south end and the other about three miles up. Both have good swimming, camping and boat launching. The Otter Valley is narrow, crowded in by steep forested mountain slopes, with a string of lakes, Otter, Frembd and Thynne, filling the valley floor. Between the lake, stretches of meadowland provide attractive settings for old ranches and some great, tumbledown barns. Above Otter Lake is Blackeyes Ranch, named after the Indian Chief who showed the fur traders the Indian trail over the mountains and who fed the hungry men with "dried carp". Blackeyes Trail, used by the Hudson's Bay Co. brigades for years, is still there in the hills southeast of Tulameen.

At Frembd Lake, where you can troll and fly-fish for small rainbows, the railway crosses the valley and squeezes the road in against a steep rock slope where, in June, brilliant clumps of mountain penstemon glow purple. Then before the broad meadows of the old Thynne Lake Ranch the railway crosses back to the east side. The white three storey ranchhouse, neatly trimmed with green, stands in a shady grove of cottonwood surrounded by red barns. Thynne's (now Cook's) was a stopping place on the 1½ day stage coach ride from Nicola to Princeton. In 1899 the stage left Nicola at 6 a.m. and reached Jack Thynne's ranch at 7 p.m. Leaving again at 6 the next morning, it reached Granite Creek at 10 and Vermilion Forks in time for lunch.

Beyond the Thynne meadows, the road runs once again through a remarkable area of steep rock scree with the creek directly below in a maze of red osier dogwood and willow. A road takes off to the right to climb up to Thalia, Goose, Lodwick and other fishing lakes. Then about 13 miles from the head of Otter Lake, Spearing Creek flows in from the west and the railway crosses the road overhead on a trestle to follow the Spearing Valley. This is marked on most maps as Thalia, a railway flagstop. The road drives northeast following Otter Creek into a tight and twisting canyon and out into open woods, bright with dandelions in early summer. Six miles from Thalia, the forest gives way to meadows and the road forks, the right hand leading a scenic six miles to Highway No. 5 south of Aspen Grove. This is the recommended route.

Signposted to Brookmere, one of the two Kettle Valley Railway towns, the left-hand road leads to Merritt by way of the Coldwater Valley. But the first part of the road is not in good condition, and it is best travelled only by those with sturdy, high-clearance vehicles. First it climbs up onto the shoulder of a mountain, then descends to Spearing Creek where it meets the railway for the journey to Brookmere, an interesting old railway town with a station and a water tower painted in shades of plum red. The store is closed and the town appears forsaken. But several of the houses are inhabited.

Logging roads, which thread through all these mountains, seem to converge on the Spearing Valley so that the road is wide and straight, though very roughly surfaced. Five miles down the hill the road and railway turn into the Coldwater Valley. The Kettle Valley Railway looped left here for the long climb up the divide to the Coquihalla Pass and down to Hope. This section of the railway has been abandoned and the trains (freight only) now run down the Coldwater to Merritt. The settlement of Kingsvale (another lovely old station) lies five miles down the Coldwater, the last point of interest along the road. From here on, the road is wide and straight and rough, a monotonous, dusty 18 miles to Merritt.

TOUR 10

Hedley High Country

Indians called it "Sna-za-ist", the Place of the Striped Rock. If you look north at the rimrocks that guard the little town of Hedley some 20 miles east of Princeton you can see the curiously crumpled strata of multi-colored cliff that prompted the name. For centuries, this was undisturbed Indian country. A trail ran along the north side of the Similkameen River to the site of Princeton where the Indians traded for the rare red earth they needed for paint. And at the village of Chuchuawa near the Striped Rock they bartered for red jasper, used for the making of fine arrowheads. The trail remains today, now a little used gravel road notable for the extraordinary number of pictographs or Indian paintings on rocks along the way. Years later, other men tramped the trail to this spot by 20 Mile Creek and found gold. Hedley and the ghost town of Nickel Plate a mile higher on the mountain both owe their existence to lode gold that was mined in such abundance for over 50 years, yielding a total of $50 million.

Travellers along Highway No. 3, which runs on the railbed of the old Great Northern Railway south of the Similkameen River, used to remember Hedley for the ruins of the gold reduction mill, a romantic tumble of shattered wood spilling down the mountainside. The ruin was considered dangerous, however, and tempting to explorers, so the property owners burned it down. From the road today there is little to see. Hedley itself, the victim of several fires, huddles quietly under the shadow of the Striped Rock; the line of the old aerial tramway still cleaves a scar line through the trees, and beside the river, tailings from the mill spread a white tableland so flat that sometimes migrating geese mistake it for a lake and land disastrously. But pause by the government "Stop of Interest" sign and follow the tramway line up two miles to the top of the mountain, then look left along the high ridges above the town. Here, perched like the ruins of an Inca city are the wooden buildings of the Mascot mine, remote and seemingly inaccessible.

In less than an hour, you can be there. You can climb the infamous "corkscrew" road to the ghost town site of Nickel Plate, then out along the ridge. It's a trip for the adventurous: the road is steep, winding and narrow, notched at times into the side of precipitous rock bluffs. Once up on the plateau, in the high, dry forest country, you can explore the mining area, drive along another cliff-hanging road to the Mascot mine ruins, or even, if you have a very rugged car, drive on over the top to Apex and down to Penticton. The backroad leaves the highway two miles east of Hedley, opposite the Indian village of Chuchuawa identified by the little white church of St. Ann's and a cluster of old, well-made log houses. In summer there are usually bluebirds here.

You'll soon find that the "corkscrew" road was well named. It twists and loops, turning back on itself in sinuous zig-zags and spiralling up through sagebrush meadows, bright in May with the gold of sunflowers and in fall with fringes of scarlet sumac. Three miles along, it traverses a rock bluff onto the shoulder of the mountain. Here, if you dare to stop, is the best view of the road, snaking up from the valley. Continue up onto the shoulder and park beside the road before the cattleguard. Walk right a little way out towards the edge for a magnificent view over the green meadows of the Similkameen Valley far below, where St. Ann's Church, dwarfed by distance, seems only a toy. This view alone is well worth the dry, dusty and sometimes scary trip.

The following five miles are less spectacular, but still fairly steep as they climb up through the forest, crossing Cahill Creek several times. The road to the townsite was built only in 1937. Before then, residents used the mine tramway or drove the mountain road 30 miles to Penticton. A signpost at a major junction points right to Nickel Plate Lake, 4 miles, Apex, 8 miles and Penticton, 28 miles. Despite the reassurances of the signpost, the road is not in good condition. Turn left here.

Gold was first found in the Similkameen River in the 1860s but this was merely a trace. In the 1890s, great mineral discoveries at Greenwood and Phoenix encouraged prospectors to search all the nearby mountains, but it was only at Hedley, far to the west, that they struck lucky. In 1898 Francis Wollaston and Constantine Arundel staked the Sunnyside, Nickel Plate, Copperfield and Bulldog claims around a rusty red outcrop where the crumbled dust around the base panned rich flakes of gold. In the fall, they took samples of the ore to the New Westminster Fair where they were studied with great interest and incredulity by M.K. Rodgers, a scout for a big U.S. mining company. Rodgers rushed to Hedley to examine the claims himself, then he made an offer for all four properties on behalf of the Marcus Daly interests from Butte, Montana. The prospectors, who did not have the money themselves to work the claims, gladly accepted the $60,000 fee.

Work on the Nickel Plate began the following year with the excavations of tunnels, the building of tote roads and camp bunkhouses. Supplies were hauled in by wagon across the mountains on the Penticton road, built in 1900, and later, ore was trundled out the same way. The properties proved so rich in gold, silver and copper that plans were made for a stamp mill at Hedley and an aerial tramway. Meanwhile, prospectors had flooded into the area and soon the whole of Nickel Plate Mountain (the new name for the Striped Rock) bristled with claim posts. The Daly Reduction Co. bought up

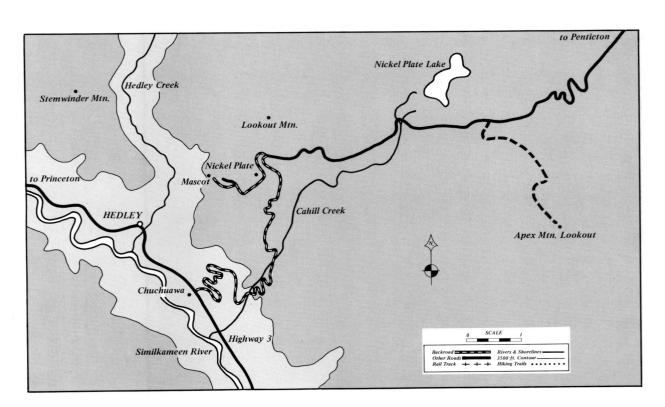

Like an Inca fortress, the ruins of Mascot Mine perch high on a rock ridge overlooking Hedley and the Similkameen Valley. Below: the infamous "corkscrew road" leading up to Nickel Plate and the mines wriggles up through sagebrush and tawny grasses. Opposite page: The road leads up onto a rock bluff, with the church of St. Ann's at the Indian village of Chuchuawa directly below.

all the claims around their own, and others that looked promising, but none proved as rich as the original ones — with one exception, the famous Mascot Fraction.

Duncan Woods from Trout Creek in the Okanagan was looking at the Nickel Plate claim maps one day as he sat in the recorder's office in Rock Creek, then the centre of the Boundary mines. He noticed a tiny piece of mountain wedged in between other claims that appeared to have been overlooked. He sent George Cahill to stake this fraction of a claim, a tiny plot on a nearly vertical cliff. And this, for its size, proved to be the richest of all, yielding nearly $9 million in gold.

Down in the valley, with the building of the mill and the two-mile long tramway, the little settlement of Hedley blossomed overnight. There were six hotels, including the grand Union, each one open 24 hours a day, seven days a week, and each one well supplied with fine cigars and the best brandy. There were two churches, a bank, a school, a newspaper, a hospital, even a golf course, in addition to stores and houses. The Welby stage provided regular service to Penticton (12 hours in an open wagon) and twice a month, gold bricks from the mill were shipped with armed escort to the Seattle assay office. High above, near the mine mouth, the townsite of Nickel Plate was established.

Many gold mines are mere flashes in the pan. The Hedley mines seemed inexhaustible. They changed owners with the years, all except the Mascot Fraction, but the gold kept coming. In 1909, the Great Northern Railway's Canadian subsidiary, the Vancouver, Victoria and Eastern, continued its line west from Oroville, Washington through Keremeos to Hedley and on to Princeton, and with better transportation, the town enjoyed a new prosperity. In 1917, however, because of war-time difficulties, the Nickel Plate mines closed. The railway, bereft of its major client, tore up the tracks between Hedley and Princeton, and the right-of-way was later taken by the highway. The mines operated again after the war and in 1937 new ore bodies were found which gave impetus to the town for another 12 years. But then the gold petered out, first at Mascot, then at Nickel Plate. Machinery was dismantled and many of the buildings were moved away. People lingered on in the Hedley townsite, but Nickel Plate on top of the corkscrew road was abandoned.

The first trace of mining activity you will meet on the road today is a huge abandoned rail-loading area (the railway dates from the 1930s). From here, roads straggle off in several directions. The uppermost road leads to the mine entrances, to tunnels and a huge high-roofed cavern cut into the mountain, the entrance perhaps to the great subterranean highway called the Dickson Incline, which linked the ore pockets by underground rail. While these tunnels appear to be hewn from solid rock, they should not be explored for they are old and subject to collapse. The lower road leads out into the open meadows of Nickel Plate townsite where only stone foundations and a few garden plants mark the locations of houses and streets. Take the road that branches left before the townsite to reach the Mascot mine. This road straggles along for several miles, ducking under an old railway trestle and climbing up the steep western ridge on a narrow one-way road notched into the cliff. Stop when you reach a wooden loading platform cantilevered out above the slope. (This platform enables you to turn around for the return trip.) The road beyond is thin and rocky and ends abruptly at a tramway terminal. It is more safely traversed on foot.

The Mascot mine buildings spill down the ridge from the road's end. A trail leads down to a long wooden stairway — use carefully, for some of the treads and siderails are missing — descending to the main cluster of weather-beaten cedar buildings poised nearly 4,000 feet above the valley floor. Explore only with the greatest caution, for all the buildings are in ruins. Further down the mountain other buildings sit in solitary splendor, unreachable.

Those attempting the cross-over to Apex and Penticton should return to the signpost and follow its directions. It's a tough eight miles; snow lingers late and may make the road impassable as late as June. Even when the snow goes, the road is wet and boggy as it circles the south end of Nickel Plate Lake. In general, turn right at all major forks except for the road signposted to Apex Mountain forestry lookout, and drive with care. The last section of road traverses a mud slide area at the base of the Apex ski lift, and from there on, it's a good road all the way to Penticton.

TOUR 11

Over Douglas Lake Range

The great billowing hills of the Nicola Valley country stretch in summer magnificently golden towards the sky. Once blanketed with bunchgrass "high as a horse's belly" they provided superb natural range for cattle and some of the miners on their way north to Cariboo gold stopped off here in the golden hills to become ranchers. Nicola country is still cattle country, its contours rounder, its mood a trifle softer than the ranchlands of the Cariboo but with the same haunting appeal. And in its heart lies Douglas Lake Ranch, one of Canada's largest and richest, named for John Douglas, a Scottish miner who homesteaded here in the 1870s. It was under a subsequent owner, "Old Danger" Greaves, that the ranch began its climb to prosperity in 1882 by supplying beef to the construction crews of the Canadian Pacific Railway, a lucrative contract, indeed. Gradually the ranch absorbed most of the neighboring homesteads and today it covers over half a million acres and runs 14,000 head of prime cattle.

From Nicola Lake, a backroad cuts through the Douglas Lake ranch to Westwold, on the highway between Vernon and Kamloops. Its 52 miles of rangeland and forest provide authentic glimpses of ranch life as they pass beside Home Ranch, the centre of Douglas Lake Cattle Co. operations. In spring, the white-faced calves are frisky beside their mothers in fields beside the road but by August all the cattle have vanished — they are up in the cool forests around Aspen Grove — and the meadows are given over to huge haying operations.

The backroad leaves Highway 5 north of Merritt, just three miles beyond the Quilchena Hotel, one of the very few old-style hotels still in operation. Three storeys high, with porches and dormer windows, the hotel was built in 1908 by speculators who believed a branch line of the CPR was coming down the valley from Kamloops to Merritt. The railway chose a different route and the hotel, a great white elegant elephant, was left advertising fine wines and hot and cold water to the wilderness. Fortunately, its position in the Nicola, one of B.C.'s less travelled valleys, has helped to preserve the hotel. It's still decked out in turn-of-the-century finery, Victorian furniture in the parlor, gaslight brackets on the walls and chamber pots in the old-fashioned bedrooms. There is even a grand old Wild West saloon, complete with bullet holes in the bar and a billiard table. The hotel is not air-conditioned, there are always plenty of mosquitoes, and you must run down the hall to use one of several communal bathrooms. But where else can you sleep in the "Ladies Parlor" or in a magnificent carved mahogany bed in the "Bridal Suite"?

From the hotel, drive north along the shores of Nicola Lake, one of the finest fishing lakes in B.C., well stocked with 6-lb rainbows, kokanee and whitefish. There's a provincial government campsite, Monck Park, on the opposite side. The backroad begins at the Quilchena Indian reserve; watch for a white-painted church and signpost to Westwold, 52 miles. The good gravel road follows the Nicola River up into hills softly rounded and bare of trees, dotted at first with clumps of sagebrush.

Opposite page: Deserted log homestead and farm machinery sit forlorn in the middle of Douglas Lake hayfields.
Top: Home Ranch, spic and span in red and white, beside a little lake called The Sanctuary.
Centre: Elegant white elephant, the Quilchena Hotel provides turn-of-the-century accommodation; stacks of hay to feed Douglas Lake beef.
Below: The dusty road to Douglas Lake and the Indian settlement of Spahomin.

In August the brown-eyed susans will still be in bloom at the road's edge, though the main floral displays take place earlier in the year. Meadowlarks and mourning doves are numerous and telephone posts along the road are favorite perching roosts for kestrels. Four miles along, a side road branches north to Glimpse Lake, 11 miles away in the hills, where fishermen can find 4-lb rainbows. Five miles further, the Indian village of Spahomin with its picturesque frame church and cluster of houses sits on a bench beside the river canyon, with a bristle of graveyard crosses white against the tawny hillside. Across the road, a deserted log homestead and barns of weather-bronzed cedar invite photography. Before the road crosses the river, the road divides, the right fork leading south to Minnie Lake and connecting trails to Pennask Lake (see Backroad No. 13). Instead, follow the signpost left across the bridge to Salmon Lake. Almost immediately, Douglas Lake appears through a fringe of scrub alder and cottonwood. Large and reed-rimmed, it reflects the opposite hills in its mirrored surface. The osprey, one of B.C.'s more unusual birds, can often be seen fishing here.

Towards the top of the lake there's an informal campsite and a B.C. government sign commemorating the Three Bar brand of the Douglas Lake Cattle Co. Three-pound rainbows and kokanee make this lake a favorite of local anglers, particularly in spring and fall. At the end of the lake, the hayfields broaden out and the road takes a refreshing dive into a shady grove of cottonwoods before emerging into Douglas Lake ranch headquarters. Home Ranch, centre of operations of this sprawling ranch, is down a short southern spur road under the welcoming wooden sign. A self-contained settlement, Home Ranch has a store, a post office, even a school, and the public is welcome to visit.

The road continues past the ranch entrance and follows the signposted route to Salmon Lake and Westwold, climbing up through rolling hills past the home of the ranch owner, "Chunky"

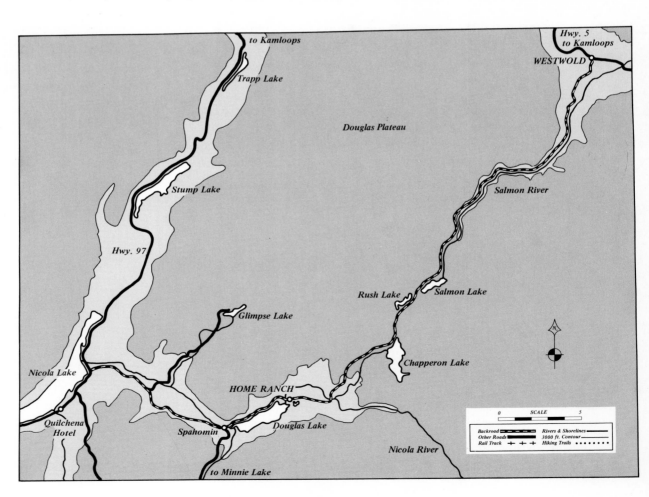

Woodward, of Woodward's Stores. From the top of the hill, look back for the best view of Home Ranch, its neat red and white buildings reflected in a little lake called The Sanctuary. After another three miles the road crosses the Nicola River and leaves its valley in search of another, winding through huge, irrigated hayfields. It passes near the north end of Chapperon Lake beside an old homestead and graveyard where the road divides again, the right fork going to Chapperon Lake Ranch, a subsidiary of Douglas Lake, and the left going on to Westwold. From here, the road which has been climbing steadily all the way from Quilchena wanders into jackpine forests and over the divide into the Salmon River valley. Salmon Lake, restricted to fly fishermen, is small but productive (rainbow to 4-lbs). There is a private fishing camp here for enthusiasts, but no public access.

The road follows the Salmon River all the way to Westwold, at first through lush watermeadows and hayfields, then as the river cuts a canyon deep into the Monte Hills, it climbs up into forest again. It was somewhere in the rugged Salmon canyon that a prospector known only as Pegleg once found a rich gold strike. He returned to San Francisco for funds, but he was taken ill and died there, unable to direct his penniless relatives to the site of his find, at least, so the story goes. Above the canyon, the road is steep, narrow and winding for several miles, but suddenly it bursts out above a little box valley, in country very different from the Douglas Lake range, with green fields and farms, cabbages and dairy cows. The valley broadens as it nears Westwold, the fields in summer purple with Canada thistle and with the ramrods of mullein beside the road. At 48 miles, just past the Lucas Ranch, the pavement begins and four miles later you are at the highway, one mile north of Westwold, with Highway 1 near Kamloops just 17 miles north.

If you are a history buff, you will know that this country was the scene of a CPR train robbery in 1906, when Bill Miner, American stage-coach highwayman who turned train bandit, held up the express at Monte Creek, then known as Ducks. Miner and his two companions were tracked to the Douglas Lake country and confronted near Chapperon Lake. Miner was tried at Kamloops and sentenced to life imprisonment at New Westminster penitentiary. He was at that time in his 60s, his health ruined by many years of imprisonment. But he tunnelled under the walls and escaped to the U.S. where he continued his career.

And it was at Westwold that the last of the Cariboo camels lived out his days, expiring finally in 1905 after 43 years of exile in B.C.

To Summerland, by way of Osprey Lake

Opposite page: Wooded seclusion on Chain Lake, one of three good fishing lakes along the road. Top: Huge A-frame barn, a landmark in the meadows, has recently disappeared. Buildings along the old Kettle Valley Railway are painted a soft plum red.

Top: The Kettle Valley Railway, now a CP freightline, crosses the road several times throug the high, flowery meadows above Princetor Log cabins, their roofs steeply pitched to war off the deep snow, sit unused beside Hayes Cree

It's not a long road, this back-country route between Princeton and Summerland, and to most people's eyes it is not as scenic as the well-travelled highway along the Similkameen River and up the Okanagan Valley. But its 60-odd miles are leisurely, without the tension of high-speed traffic. You can stop just about anywhere to pick wildflowers, listen to the birds or cast a fishing line into a stream. It's also a road for railway buffs for it follows the line of the old Kettle Valley Railway, now a CPR freight line. And this explains those non-existent settlements shown on most maps, Jura, Jellicoe, Bankeir, Demuth and Faulder — improbable names, reminiscent of Gilbert and Sullivan operas. They are merely flag stops on the railway.

On fur-trader Archibald McDonald's map of the Thompson Country dated 1827 this road from Princeton to the Okanagan Valley was called Indian Road but it was never a major transportation route until the Kettle Valley Railway chose to come this way from Summerland in 1915. To find the road, take the Merritt road (Highway No. 5) north from Princeton, over the Tulameen River bridge. At the top of the hill, fork right along the road signposted to Hedley. The Summerland road (known locally as Five Mile Road) branches left off this almost immediately to Sunflower Downs, the Princeton racetrack and Osprey Lake. (The Hedley road itself, an old Indian trail, and later the Dewdney Road, runs along the north side of the Similkameen River, a good backroad alternative to the highway.)

The high country above Princeton is open and grassy, rolling rangeland dotted with lakes and stands of pine. In spring it's a good place for waterbirds: teal, grebe, phalarope and various kinds of duck haunt the upland lakes. May covers the hills with balsam root sunflowers, but other flowers are generally at their best in early July which spreads a multi-colored shag rug of wild geranium, lupin, brown-eyed susan, scarlet gilia, creamy wild buckwheat and dozens of others. When the road leaves the upland meadows for the forested creekside, flower lovers can find fireweed, Indian paintbrush, tiger lilies, columbines, larkspur, wild roses and, on the rocky road edges, masses of yellow stonecrop. At the Okanagan end of the road, there are bitterroot and milkweed and other dry belt blooms.

Three miles or so up from the junction, a side road leads left to join Highway 5 at Allison Creek, north of Princeton. This is the route the railway takes on its climb up to the plateau, recrossing the road half a dozen times to gain elevation. An obscure hand-painted sign 2½ miles further along leads down a grassy overgrown track to Jura, now just two or three deserted cedar barns and a group of red railway sheds. Jura was named, according to the CPR, after a mountain range in Austria, presumably by a homesick settler.

Soon after Jura, the road leaves the ranchlands of the plateau and switchbacks steeply down to Hayes Creek, which it follows for the next 11 miles. From here, the road goes through forests most of the way, with occasionally a clearing of ranchland or water meadow. At the bottom of the hill is a fine two-storey log house, and a little way beyond, two small log barns sit in an unkempt field on the lip of the river, their hand-split cedar shake roofs steep and etched with moss. This road is a particularly good one for "collectors" of old barns, although the most magnificent one of all, a giant open A-frame some 30 feet high, has recently been removed.

Since leaving the plateau, the Kettle Valley Railway has been out of sight. The Hayes Creek valley is a narrow one, and the few places where it widens out have either been taken up by ranches or are filled by lakes, and the railway takes a higher route on the mountain side. A break in the forest brings you to the Triangle K Ranch, a wide triangular meadow which seems to have been subdivided for recreational lots. About 17 miles down the road from Jura, there's a sign pointing reassuringly to Summerland, and this is the only clue to the whereabouts of Jellicoe. You have just passed it.

Chain Lake, the first of four in the valley, is about 20 miles from Princeton and was restocked in 1973 with rainbows. The southern rim is ringed with summer cabins and on a fine summer week-end the lake surface is dotted with fishermen in boats of all kinds. The unofficial campsite between the road and the lake is usually full, for it's a popular spot. Just beyond the lake, a private side road goes north to Tepee Lakes for good rainbow fishing. The buildings beside the road are a base camp

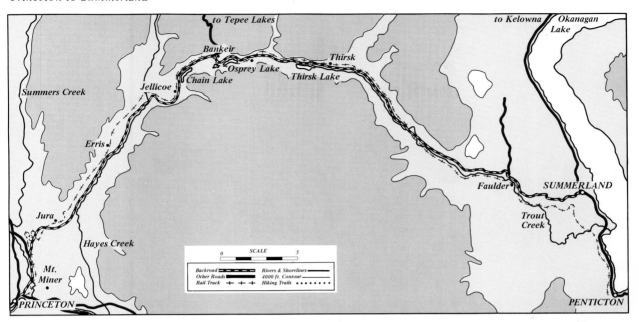

for a popular fishing lodge on the lakes and constitute the "settlement" of Bankeir. Here the railway crosses the road and takes the southern route around Osprey Lake. Link Lake, the smallest of the chain, lies hidden from the road, but offers rainbows to 4 lbs. On both Link and Osprey there are recreational settlements, with some lots (in 1975) still for sale.

Beyond Osprey Lake, the railway crosses the road again and this crossing marks the divide at 3,500 feet. Soon the road and railway pick up the Trout Creek valley for the run down to Summerland, passing the abomination of Trout or Thirsk Lake, which was dammed without the land being cleared first; drowned trees rim the lake with an ugly grey stubble, ruining all possibilities of recreational use. Trout Creek valley is a steep one, really a canyon; the railway at Demuth (you have passed Thirk already) follows the river down into the canyon, crossing it on several high trestles, but the road keeps high on the hillside, emerging soon into dry Okanagan uplands. Here there are stands of Ponderosa pine and sagebrush, with pink-flowered milkweed beside the road in summer. Soon you will come to an intersection with a wider road coming down from the Darke Lake-Prairie Valley area. Turn right here and soon you are at Faulder, yet another flag station on the Kettle Valley Railway, named after the pioneer settler in the area who came to Summerland in 1891. Unlike some of the other places along the line, Faulder was more than just a whistle stop. It had a sawmill, a school, and several ranches. From Faulder it's less than three miles to pavement and the run down into the orchards to Summerland.

TOUR 13

Over the Hills to Minnie Lake

If you study a large scale map of the Nicola Valley, in particular the southeast corner, you will see that the road from Quilchena to Pennask Lane traverses a large hillocky plateau, splashed with the blue of lakes, that bears the name of "Commonage Reserve". This unromantic name does not do justice to the high country, for it would be difficult to find an area more uncommonly beautiful. An undulating sweep of grassland, lupine blue in summer, with little lakes and drifts of trees in the hollows, it's a country that urges exploration. On ripe summer evenings, when the valley below is already in shade, up here the grass is golden in the sunset, the shadows long, giving the rounded curves of the hills a slumbering, human quality. Meadowlarks trill their rich warm songs as if they have much to say before the light fades and along the meandering road a scurrying army of the smaller horned larks is forever in retreat.

If when you left the highway you expected, as many people do, to climb up into forests like those that clothe the Okanagan hills, the wide open grasslands will be a revelation. Here, on the western rim of the plateau, there is a sense of sky that you associate more with the Prairies or the sagebrush benches of the Cariboo than with Nicola country. But it's only a momentary respite. Look eastwards and you can see the dark forests approaching; drive a few miles and you will be immersed in them.

The road from Quilchena to Pennask Lake and Peachland is the only one linking the Nicola and Okanagan Valleys and it could be a useful backroad shortcut. Ten miles of this crossover, beyond Minnie Lake, is in execrable condition, narrow, wet, potholed and rocky, and requires either a four-wheel drive or a sturdy car with high clearance, which puts it beyond the range of most back-country drivers. Beyond Minnie Lake the forest closes in and the road is wooded all the way to Peachland. If you want to keep to the beautiful rangeland of the "commonage", you can instead circle back to your starting point by way of Douglas Lake.

North of Merritt on Highway No. 5 lies the cluster of buildings that goes by the name of Nicola. Once the most important town in the valley, Nicola was ignored by the railway which went instead to Merritt in 1907 and took most businesses with it. Nicola lapsed slowly into a state of semi-decline. Though people live there still, it is only a shadow of a town. There are no gas stations, no motels, no shops, nothing to hamper the atmosphere of the turn of the century. Prominent is Murray United Church built in 1876, a diminutive frame building painted a spanking white with a huge bell in its turret. Its graveyard with leaning headstones of carved white marble is worth a visit — as are all graveyards if you have a feeling for history and the continuity of things. Opposite lies an imposing turreted mansion and further along the street is the old courthouse, its once imposing driveway now a family lawn. Enough remains to flesh out the memories of Nicola, the oldest of the valley towns, on the fur trade route between Hope and Kamloops. It is now headquarters for the Nicola Lake Cattle Ranch.

Nicola, the lake, river and town, were named after local Indian chief N'Kwala, who was born in the 1780s. John Tod, Hudson's Bay Co. trader at Kamloops, described him as "a very great chieftain and a bold man, for he had 17 wives".

Ten miles north of Nicola, beside the lake, is the Quilchena Hotel, a landmark since 1908 (see Backroad Tour 11). Take the first right turn about a mile beyond the hotel, signposted to Minnie, Paradise and Pennask Lakes. If you stopped long enough at the Quilchena Hotel to read some of the old guest book pages that decorate the walls, Minnie Lake will be familiar as the home of a Mr. J. Raspberry, a frequent visitor in the hotel's early years. The road climbs steeply up through dry country, with sagebrush and prickly pear cactus and the brilliant yellow tufts of rabbit bush in August. Soon there's a fine view down to the deep U-shaped trough of Nicola Lake. As the road climbs higher through stands of yellow pine the soil cover changes from sagebrush to grass and where the land dips into a hollow, the grass is greener, a pleasant contrast to the brown and the gold of the summer hills. Ten miles up and it's a gentle roller-coaster road that seems to go on forever towards the eastern hills. Twelve miles and there's the first of the lakes, an irregular dimple with a marsh of pink-tinged grass at one end and a speckling of waterbirds. Another mile and there's a sign (alas, badly disfigured by hunters' bullets) marking the boundary of Minnie Lake Bird Sanctuary.

On the shore of Minnie Lake a public campground has been provided by the Nicola Valley Rod & Gun Club and the Douglas Lake Cattle Co. for the lake is a popular destination for anglers who come in pursuit of 10-lb. rainbows, though the lake is subject to winter kill. The lake is also a good spot for shorebirds, and there is always a swarm of swallows here to eat the mosquitoes, the plague of the lakes. Keep a watch for hawks and coyotes.

Beyond the lake are hayfields, snake fences and corrals, for this is cattle country, though you may not see any in summer when they are driven to the high forests. Those willing to try the road to Pennask Lake should turn left past Minnie Lake and continue beside another lake, unnamed on the government maps. This seems more popular than Minnie with campers; perhaps the fish are bigger or the mosquitoes less troublesome. Certainly in summer the edges beside the road are thickly clustered with flowers, small, pale purple thistles, yellow knapweed and wild white barley. At the lake's end are a few old shacks, some rusted relics of cars and heaps of shattered timbers, remnants of a sawmill. Duck under an elevated irrigation flume, through a stand of aspen and you're into the forest and ready for those rough 10 miles. Once at Pennask Lake, the road improves, passing some fine abandoned log homesteads before joining the oiled superhighway coming down from the Brenda mine for the easy swoop down into the orchards of Peachland.

Most travellers, however, should turn back after they have explored the lakes, and take the right hand fork just north of Minnie Lake. This road rambles across the top of the plateau, past hayfields and duck-filled potholes to Douglas Creek in its fringe of pine and birch. In spring or fall, this section of road is likely to be wet and slippery. It's a 10-mile ride from Minnie Lake to the western edge of Douglas Lake, which you can see as soon as you begin the descent. Below, its turreted church a landmark, is the Indian village of Spahomin, on the opposite side of the Nicola River.

As you near Spahomin, keep a look out for old log cabins. One of them near here was the scene of a shootout back in the 1870s. The three McLean brothers, half-breed sons of a Kamloops fur trader, and their cousin, Alex Hare, were only in their early teens when they murdered a constable and a shepherd. After a desperate manhunt, they holed up in one of the cabins beside the creek where they were besieged by a posse of ranchers. After a couple of gun fights the boys surrendered, mostly because of hunger and thirst and cold, and later all four went to the gallows at New Westminster. The cabin is not identified. You can make your own choice.

When you reach Spahomin, turn right for a visit to the great Douglas Lake Cattle ranch, or left onto a good gravel road that follows Nicola River down to the lake on Highway 5, a few miles north of where you started.

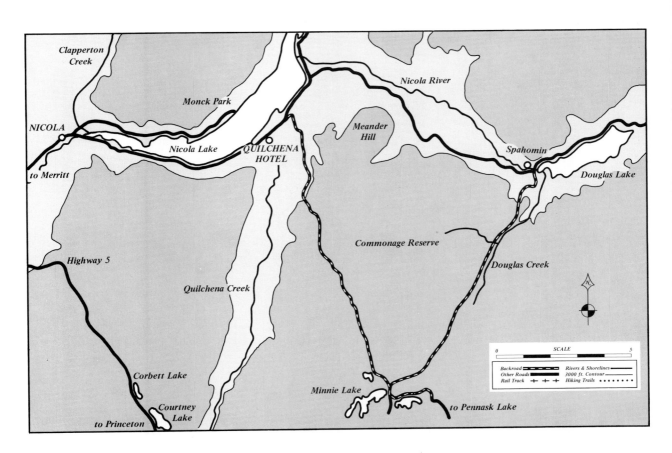

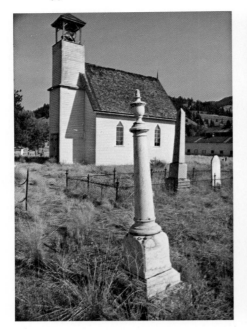

The high rolling grasslands of Minnie Lake are bright with lupines in spring, wild barley and purple thistle in August. Coyotes prowl the dry hills. Far left: Murray United Church and historic graveyard at Nicola; cactus blossoms and a log barn on the Pennask Lake end of the road.

TOUR 14

Bridesville Detour

From the desert oasis town of Osoyoos by the warmest freshwater lake in Canada, the highway route east leaves the valley of the Okanagan and grinds laboriously up into the dry pine forest of Anarchist Mountain, reaching the summit at 3,700 feet. From there, a long series of swoops and curves plummets the traveller down to the little town of Rock Creek, where the stream of that name tumbles into the Kettle River. The only settlement along this scenic stretch of Highway No. 3 is Bridesville, a single short street lying parallel to the highway. Its name is one of the prettiest in B.C., but the village itself is not particularly pretty, just a string of little houses, a garage, school, store and post office.

Bridesville used to be memorable for a romantic old frame homestead standing forlorn in the middle of a field north of the highway, its wood weathered to a deep burnt brown and its front porch jauntily askew. Alas, in the spring of 1975 it was gone, a clearing in the meadow and a pile of old lumber marking its grave. Soon, that too, was gone. And Bridesville will never be the same.

Bridesville was first called "Maud" after the wife of Hozie Edwards, the area's first settler and later the first postmaster. Between the border settlement of Osoyoos and the gold camp of Rock Creek it was a stop for freighters on the long haul over Anarchist, but it never amounted to much until 1905 when the Vancouver, Victoria and Eastern Railway routed its tracks through the area on its way from Midway to Oroville. Bridesville, as a station on the line, immediately became important. In 1907 a Canadian customs post opened here. In 1910, David McBride, after whom the settlement had been renamed, built the grand Bridesville Hotel, hauling its bar from the Bucket of Blood saloon in deserted Camp McKinney up on Baldy Mountain. This bar was of solid tamarack, its front of whipsawn lumber, its top a hand-hewn slab, and there was a huge ornate mirror. Later, McBride added a dance hall to the hotel, and additional rooms were built. Business was brisk in this lively railway town. Settlement increased in the rolling grass hills around. Soon there were a score of farms and homesteads, even a school. For 20 years the area thrived. Then changing patterns of transportation and a recession in the Boundary mines forced the VV&E Railway, a subsidiary of the Great Northern, to cancel its service. Bridesville and its neighbor Sidley down the line were suddenly no longer on the railway map. Sidley, an old mining town, gave up the ghost for good but Bridesville survived, the nucleus of a thriving farm community. The grand hotel and its notorious saloon bar closed with the railway, along with many of the other establishments. Bridesville the railway town is difficult to imagine now. Even the railway itself has vanished although today's main street was built on the right-of-way, as the line wound up the hill from Baker Creek.

From Bridesville, a short backroad curves southeast to take a meandering tour through the farmlands of Rock Mountain. This makes a good alternative to the highway which it rejoins at Rock Creek. Maps show this road turning off the highway at the west end of the Bridesville street. This steep route has been replaced by a new road that leaves the highway a short distance east, then cuts back under the ledge on which the town stands, crossing Baker Creek through a marshy area with red-wing blackbirds noisy in the cat-tails. On the other side of the creek, the road plunges into forest for its climb up Rock Mountain, once called One-Eyed Mountain because the first three settlers, de Landers, Bozarth and Wilder, all miners, were all one-eyed. What a pity the name was changed!

Nearly three miles from Bridesville the little white-painted frame church of the Sacred Heart sits in a forest clearing, its doorway shaded by a tall evergreen. Most of the abandoned wooden churches in the Interior are Indian, but this was built in the 1920s by the three Dumont brothers, Paul, Joe and Hugo, who came to the Bridesville area from France in the 1880s. The graveyard is empty except for a fenced-off area containing three graves, two of them unnamed and marked only by wooden crosses and the other of Stanley Dumont, who was killed in 1943 on a RCAF training flight.

The road continues, diving in and out of forest and into clearings of rolling hills with farms and homesteads, deserted cabins and even a couple of little lakes along the way. At one white farm house pigs snorted in a field beside the road; at others there were cows and chicken and white domestic geese. A farmer ploughed his hillside field in shallow ridges while up on the hill, the original two-storey log homestead, still in good exterior repair, is used as a cow shed. Another farm groups its buildings around a blue pond and away in the distance, above a fringe of trees, the snow cone of Mount Baldy with its ski trails shone white, an idyllic, picture postcard view. The road's gravel surface is well-maintained (the school buses use it) and the drive, though short — a mere 14 miles — is pleasantly rural and best of all, quiet.

Twelve miles along, the road divides, left (north) to the highway at Rock Creek two miles down the hill, and right along a private road that dead-ends at the U.S. boundary, 3½ miles further south. This road leads through the Harpur Ranch, one of the oldest in the area (1862), scenically situated beside gurgling Myers Creek. But before the ranch, the road curves around Myers Lake which must be one of the most popular spots in the province for yellow-headed blackbirds. Birding groups come often to the lake, with permission from the Harpurs, for day outings. The maps show a townsite at the international boundary and a road leading across to Chesaw, Washington. But the town which once had a hotel, school and several houses has vanished and the border crossing is closed. All that

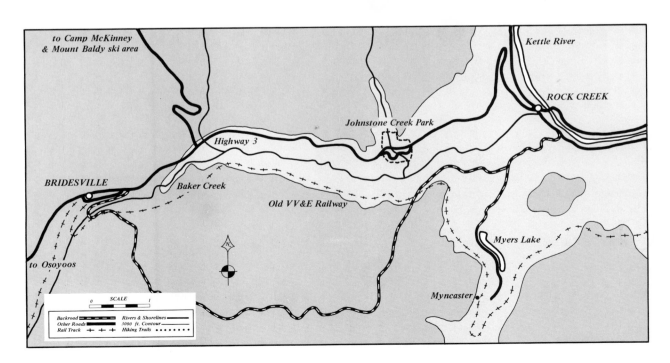

Left: Abandoned homestead in field just north of the highway at Bridesville was pulled down in the spring of 1975.
Top: Deserted cabin and farm truck, killed by target shooters. Above: High grasslands of Anarchist Mountain.

remains of Myncaster is the Canadian Customs house, now a small ranch house.

As you might have guessed, the non-existent town of Myncaster was another victim of the railway closure. The VV&E Railway came up Myers Creek from Midway, looped around the valley on a high trestle to Myncaster, then went on around Rock Mountain to Bridesville. Myncaster was named for the McMynn brothers, original owners of the Harpur Ranch (the water licence on the creek was granted in 1862). W.G. McMynn was provincial constable at Midway at the time of the Camp McKinney holdup of 1896, a notorious event in its day. His brother, Thomas was later killed while leading a packtrain of horses over the lake crossing at Osoyoos and his gravestone is to be seen on a bluff east of Myers Creek just beyond the Harpur Ranch. If you wish to explore the Myers Creek valley, the ghost of Myncaster and the railway, ask permission at the Harpur Ranch, then retrace your steps to the junction and continue to the end of the backroad trail at Rock Creek.

Rock Creek is one of the oldest settlements on the B.C. mainland, founded in 1859 when Canadian Adam Beam recorded the first claim on this placer gold creek. Two years later, 500 miners were working the creek and another 100 or so prospecting on Boundary, Myers and Cedar Creek. Most of the miners were Americans from California and supplies came north up the Kettle and Sanpoil Rivers from Spokane. The gold discovery at Rock Creek was the impetus that Governor James Douglas needed to push through a Canadian supply route from the Coast into the southern Interior, and Edgar Dewdney, a 24-year-old English engineer was given the task of building first a trail, then a wagon route across the mountains from Hope. On August 30, 1860, Charles Wilson, secretary of the British Boundary Commission which was then surveying the 49th parallel, reported in Rock Creek "a good many substantial log buildings, stores, gambling houses, grog shops, butcher's shops etc. and a good supply of everything". Governor Douglas himself visited the "city" in the same year, appointed George Cox gold commissioner and sent for John Haynes from Osoyoos as customs officer.

Ironically, by the time the Dewdney Trail reached Rock Creek in the fall of 1861, Rock Creek gold was all but played out. Miners were leaving by droves in hopes of easier gold on Mission Creek in the Okanagan. By November, Rock Creek was deserted.

Today, a government picnic site and plaque by the Rock Creek bridge commemorate the site of old Rock Creek, one of the most famous placer gold creeks in the province, earning an estimated $250,000 in gold in less than two years. The stream was reworked in the 1890s and again in the 1930s. Rock Creek was also an old Indian camp location. A set of pictographs on the north side of the river is worth searching for.

From Rock Creek, Highway No. 33 leads north through Beaverdell and Carmi to Kelowna, and Highway No. 3 leads east to Midway, Greenwood and Grand Forks. Or you can head back along the highway to Bridesville, where you started.

Top: Mount Baldy gleams white above forests and hill farms near Bridesville. Above: The frame church of the Sacred Heart on Rock Mountain. Sturdy log farmhouse, now used as a cowshed, sits forlorn in the middle of a newly ploughed field.

TOUR 15

Okanagan Escape Route

When summer tourists fill the resorts of the South Okanagan and highways along the lakes are jammed with traffic, it's good to know that there are backroads nearby where you can enjoy the hush of the countryside. A small pocket of backcountry, wedged between the towns of Oliver, Okanagan Falls and Keremeos and bordered by Highways 97 and 97A, manages to keep intact its feeling of quiet isolation in spite of easy access from several directions. Its roads all lead by their own devious ways to the great sagebrush bowl of White Lake, where the Dominion Radio Astrophysical Observatory fishes the sky for radio signals from outer space. It's because of the observatory that this area is so tranquil, for development has been restricted so that the scientific equipment can operate without radio interference.

Perhaps the most interesting route begins at Oliver and crosses over to Highway 97A by way of Twin Lakes. Only 20 miles long, it nevertheless needs a full half day to be enjoyed thoroughly. Take the Fairview Road north from Oliver — it turns westwards up the hill past the hospital — and follow it through neat residential streets onto orchard benches and higher still onto a sagebrush plateau above the valley. This is the site of Fairview, the Okanagan's most famous gold-mining town which shone brightly but briefly around the turn of the century and today has vanished almost without trace. A B.C. government Stop of Interest sign is its only gravestone, except for a solitary log jail-house which stands at a tilt beside it.

Lode gold in the hills behind Fairview gave substance to the town as early as 1887 when the famous Stemwinder claim was discovered. Later other claims were staked and mined. Morning Star, Tin Horn, Wildhorse, Smuggler, Brown Bear and Rattler, rollicking names that foretold of a lively settlement. Hotels and saloons soon sprouted lustily among the sagebrush. In 1892, the two-storey Golden Gate opened its doors, the first of six hotels to grace the mining town. Later followed the Miner's Rest, Moffat's Saloon in the gulch above, the Blue House, the Second Golden Gate known familiarly as the "Fish House" because the cook always served fish on Fridays and, most impressive of all, Hotel Fairview, an elegant three-storey building with a gothic tower that prompted its nickname, "The Big Tepee". The first buildings snuggled close to the waters of Reed Creek where the mines were, but as these expanded — at one time five were operating their own stamp mills — a townsite was surveyed on the flats below the gulch. Here, in addition to the hotels, sprang up two churches, two livery stables, a blacksmith's shop, government house, jail, drug store, Chinese laundry and sundry stores and houses, only one of which, the J.R. Brown house, survives. It can be found on the eastern edge of the flats, south of the jail. Stage coaches provided service to Camp McKinney, Penticton and south to the U.S. town of Oro, now Oroville. The population swelled to more than 500. A diptheria epidemic and a disastrous fire which levelled the Hotel Fairview seemed only momentary setbacks. But by 1906, the veins of ore in the gulch were giving out and one by one, the mines closed. Four years later, Fairview was finished. The townsfolk moved away.

Deserted buildings in the dry Okanagan air don't rot but they burn like kindling. A few of the Fairview buildings were moved down the hill to the new settlement of Oliver and the rest went up in flames. The jail, the Brown house and Moffat's Saloon in the gulch are all that is left of the glamorous town. The only gold comes these days from sunflowers blazing on the hills in May and the golden notes of the meadowlarks which capture the satisfaction of summer in their cheery songs.

To see some of the mining relics, continue straight along the road that follows the creek into the forested gulch. This eventually goes over the shoulder of Orofino Mountain and down Blind Creek to the settlement of Cawston near Keremeos. A more interesting road, signposted to the Oliver dump, turns right at the middle of the Fairview townsite. This snakes along a narrow valley, beaded with ponds and fringed with stands of Ponderosa pine. Three miles along, a road turns left to Burnell Lake, a good fishing spot, while the road coming in from the southwest a few miles further on leads back to the Okanagan Valley near Inkaneep Provincial Park, an excellent little wooded campsite where the birdwatching is particularly good. This road is generally considered to be the original route of the fur brigade through the Okanagan. The trail left the valley near Oliver and took an upland route across the White Lake bowl, up Marron Valley, along Shingle Creek and Garnet Valley to Peachland. Meyers Flats, the meadows which begin a mile or so beyond the junction, must have provided good grazing for the fur traders' horses.

The Meyers Flats area is one of the few places in B.C. where you can see the poor-wills, birds like huge, strangely mottled moths that crouch beside the road at night in search of insects. Similar in looks to a nighthawk, only smaller and with rounded wings, the poor-wills can often be spotted

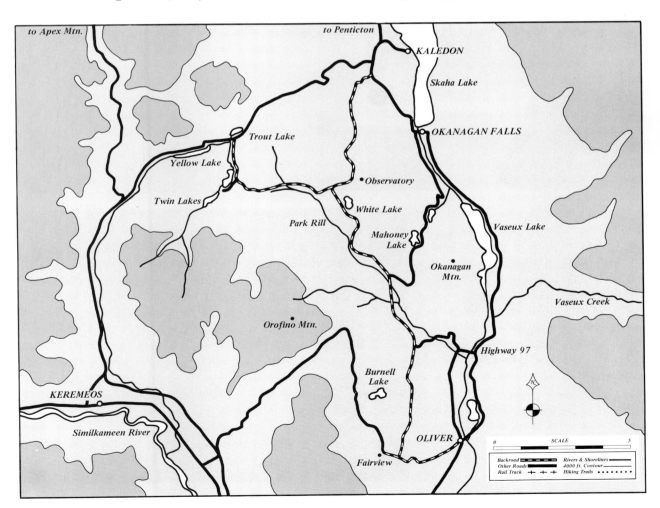

Sunset over White Lake: the great sagebrush bowl is hushed, the long-billed curlews call and coyote howl in the hills. Right: reed patterns in Green Lake.

Top: The scanning eye of the White Lake Radio Astrophysical Observatory by the alkaline lake. Middle: Fairview jail, one of the few relics of the gold town above Oliver. Sunflowers spangle the hillsides above. Below: Mountain bluebell and yellow fritillary bloom early among White Lake sagebrush.

when car headlights turn their eyes to glowing rubies. If you stop the car, the birds will often allow you to approach quite close before they flutter off. Their night cry is unmistakable, a lonely "poor-will" echoing among the arid hills.

Beyond Meyers Flats, a farmhouse stands at the junction of yet another road, signposted right to Green Lake. This winds down by Mahoney and Green Lakes to Okanagan Falls. Recreational home lots are currently (1975) for sale. Turn left at the junction and continue past farm meadows and into woods beside a trickling creek. Then the road rounds a tight corner by some rock bluffs and climbs out beside Dry Lake, in summer merely an alkaline patch of earth, and into the White Lake basin, an expansive area of rolling sagebrush hills. Although not high in elevation, the hills host some of the flowers more used to alpine terrain. In April, look for the soft, purple-blue trumpet clusters of mertensia or mountain bluebell and the solitary yellow bells of the shy fritillary. In June the hillsides may be hazy with the soft purple of phacelia, and later, the elegant pinkish-white Lewisia will be in bloom. It's cactus country, too, so wear sturdy shoes for walking, and keep a sharp look out for rattlesnakes.

The White Lake bowl, a dry and dusty spot in summer, is a nesting ground for long-billed curlews. If you stop here and wait quietly beside the road you will probably see them flying overhead and hear their plaintive, unearthly calls. When Europeans first discovered this spot, the hills were richly clothed in bunchgrass and cattle were grazed here. By 1923, Charles Camsell's geological survey showed that already the grass had been replaced by sage, a sign of overgrazing. He also recorded a post office here, six miles west of Okanagan Falls, and charted the six-square-mile deposit of coal-bearing rock which had been discovered earlier and used by the smithy at Fairview.

The South Okanagan Collieries Ltd. staked the coalfields in 1921, and began development five years later. The coal was sulphurous, production was small and the company folded. Two miners from Princeton sank a new shaft in 1933, found a four-foot seam of clean coal, and sold 110 tons in Penticton. Since then, the coal mines of White Lake have been abandoned.

White Lake itself is indeed white, a shallow alkaline lake which nevertheless attracts waterbirds in spring and fall. The great metal scanner of the observatory and its long wires strung on poles in a symmetrical grid seem out of place on this lonely moorland. The observatory is open to the public on Sundays in July and August only, from 2 to 5 p.m.

From the observatory, roads lead northeast to Highway 97 south of Kaleden, and west around the other rim of the sagebrush bowl, past White Lake Ranch and down Park Rill valley to Twin Lakes. Turn right at the lakes junction for the easy journey back to the highway, about a mile north of Yellow Lake.

TOUR 16

In Search of McKinney Gold

T he road linking the two gold mining ghost towns of Fairview in the Okanagan above Oliver and Camp McKinney on the shoulder of Mount Baldy looks easy enough to follow on the British Columbia one-inch to two-miles map (issued in 1973). There's a good stretch of "loose surface, main" road at one end and "loose surface, secondary" at the other. But the 10 miles in between will more than likely give trouble. For the former stage coach route has been muddled and confused by a maze of logging roads; upkeep seems poor and signposts nonexistent. Several of the creek bridges are in precarious condition and at least one of the creeks must be forded. Intrepid drivers with four-wheel drive vehicles or sturdy cars with high clearance stand a chance of completing the crossover; others are advised to stay clear. Nevertheless the road is definitely worth travelling, even if you have to drive the two ends separately, leaving out the 10-mile difficult section in the middle. For somewhere along the way is a cache of gold bars worth nearly $100,000!

Fairview (see Backroad Number 15) on a high bench overlooking the south Okanagan Valley, was born in 1887 with the discovery of lode gold in nearby hills. Two years later, with mines such as Stemwinder, Morning Star, Brown Bear and Joe Dandy in roaring production, the town was a bustling metropolis, with laid out streets, hotels, saloons and stores. It was connected by stage to Oroville, Washington, to the south, and Camp McKinney, another gold town over the hills to the east. This town, high under the summit of Mount Baldy, was founded in the same year as Fairview and grew fast. In 1896 it had several saloons, including one that went by the lugubrious name of The Bucket of Blood, boarding houses for the miners, and stores. The stamp mill of the Cariboo-Amelia mine operated 24 hours a day and gold bullion was shipped regularly to the San Francisco mint. There were two roads to McKinney: the Sidley road from Anarchist Mountain where Robert Sidley from Ontario established the first homestead on Nine-Mile Creek and the road from Fairview up Wolfcub Creek and through the forest. Meyerhoff's stage coaches provided regular service along the Sidley Road to Midway and Halls Line stages ran the Fairview route. The roads converged about two miles from Camp McKinney.

In August, 1896, George McCaulay, one of the Cariboo-Amelia shareholders, tossed three gold bars into a gunny sack and loaded up his buckboard for the journey to Midway. He had made the trip several times before and apparently thought little of it. Two miles from camp he was held up by a masked man who stepped out from bushes beside the road brandishing a rifle. He ordered McCaulay to throw down the bullion and keep going. McCaulay complied, then raced eight miles to the Hozier Farm. Here, he persuaded 12-year-old Leonard Hozier to ride back to the camp to raise the alarm, while he went on to report the theft to constables Dinsmore and McMynn at Midway. A posse was organized but no trace of the highwayman was found. Only the discarded sack and two empty whisky bottles remained at the scene of the holdup.

Top: Chief Louie's log barn in tangled summer meadows at old Wolftown. Right: Hay meadows at McCuddy's, once a stage coach stop on the route from Fairview to Camp McKinney.

Mining ghosts of Camp McKinney near the Mount Baldy ski area. Below: the road winds through forests bright with lupines and scarlet gilia in summer, but confusing to the traveller because of many unmarked logging roads.

Investigations continued and suspicion fell on miner Matt Roderick, who had reported sick on the day of the robbery and left camp by stage a few days afterwards to return to his home in Tacoma, Washington. Roderick was reputedly a quiet man, a non-smoker and non-drinker, but he had a passion for gambling. On paydays he would play cards non-stop till all his money was gone. When he left Camp McKinney he was, as usual, penniless. He borrowed money from a friend for his stage fare home and all he carried was his bedroll. Once home, however, Roderick started spending. He paid off the taxes on his house and began gambling again. Pinkerton detectives, hired by the mine owners, watched his every move, believing that he might have smuggled out the smallest of the three gold bricks in his bedroll and that sooner or later he would return to Camp McKinney to retrieve the others. There was no other reason for his returning to the mine. Before he left, he had been told flatly that he would not be hired there again.

In October that year, word reached Camp McKinney that Roderick was on the move. He had been seen riding south of Oroville on a fine grey horse. Indian scouts posted along the trails later reported him approaching the gold camp from the west. Mine superintendent Joseph Keane and R.W. Deans set off down the Fairview road, planning to bring Roderick in for questioning. Through the thickening gloom of that fall evening they caught up with a man leading a horse. Deans stepped cautiously into the bushes but Keane shouted out, "Is that you, Matt?" There was no answer. A moment later, so Deans testified, a shot rang out and Roderick fell to the ground, shot through the heart. Keane later said, "I had to do it or he would have shot me".

Roderick, who was walking away from Camp McKinney when he was shot, supposedly had already retrieved the cached gold. But his saddle bags were empty. Only a few dollars and two small chips of gold were found in his pockets. His rifle was plugged up with grease rags and his six-shooter was rusty — as if they had been buried somewhere. At the inquest, held in Greenwood the following day, the coroner called the killing justifiable homicide and closed the case. The provincial police were more particular. Keane was tried, found guilty of manslaughter and sentenced to *one day* in prison (which he had already served)!

If indeed Roderick was the highwayman, why was he leaving Camp McKinney empty handed? Did he return just to retrieve his weapons? Did he have an accomplice? Why was Keane so quick to shoot? These questions will never be answered. The chances are that the gold bars are still in hiding somewhere along the McKinney Road, and who knows, if you stop often along the trail and poke around in the forest, you might just be the one to find them.

The stagecoach route begins at Fairview. Follow Fairview Road west from the centre of Oliver for about two miles up to a sagebrush flat. There is little here today to remind you of the gold town. Only the little log jail remains, and further up in the gulch the relics of Moffat's Saloon molder in the woods. Even the cemetery is difficult to find. Return to Oliver and continue east across the highway along the McKinney Road which crosses the Okanagan River. Take the right fork at the next street junction and drive past the new hospital over a bumpy cattleguard and straight ahead onto a gravel road where a big colorful sign declares the entrance to the Inkaneep Indian Reserve.

Once into Indian reserve, the lush irrigated fruitlands of the South Okanagan are left behind and the road climbs through arid benchlands with sagebrush, sumac and creosote bush and a few Ponderosa pines, following Wolfcub Creek up into the hills. Five miles along, a white house sheltering behind a screen of poplars has "Chief Louie" written proudly across its face. Here, there used to be an Indian settlement called Wolftown because of the wolves that roamed the hills. Now there is just the house and a beautiful old log barn sitting in summer in a tousled meadow of long golden grass, with chokecherry bushes keeping off the dust from the road behind. The hill above was known for many years as "Black Mary's Hill" and her grave used to be beside the road nearby. Who Black Mary was has been forgotten, and her grave has vanished.

From Chief Louie's, the road climbs higher through the rolling uplands and as elevation increases, trees close in, the air becomes cooler and pine fresh. In summer there are clumps of golden gaillardia or Indian blanket flower beside the road, and wild blue asters and mariposa lilies in the

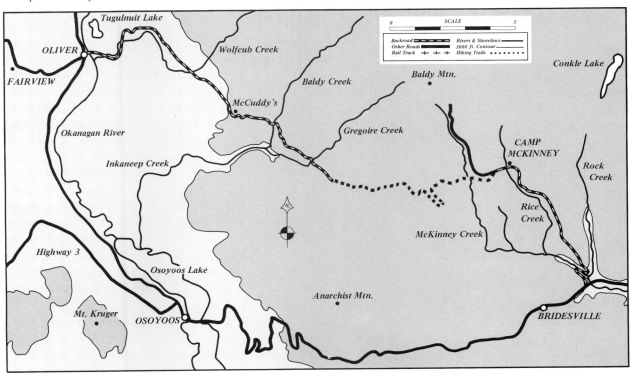

woods. Four miles beyond Chief Louie's the road crosses McCuddy Creek and into the cleared farmland of the old McCuddy Ranch. The McCuddys settled here in 1893, and soon their modest homestead was expanded into a 40-room stopping house for trade on the McKinney Road, with bunkhouses and stables for 100 horses.

Apart from the McCuddy property and a few other farm clearings, the McKinney road is mostly a forest road, cool and green with inviting clear water creeks. At first, all the creeks are named (Baldy and Gregoire both have excellent drinking water and make good picnic spots) and there are signposts to keep you on the McKinney Road. Unhappily, this does not last. Shortly after crossing Gregoire Creek, the road deteriorates, changing on the map to "rough". Most travellers should turn back here. But with patience and a good map, plus a sturdy vehicle, it should be possible to thread your way through the remaining 10 miles to Camp McKinney, providing all creek bridges are still passable. After four miles you should hit the power line, then loop sharply southwards for a mile to cross one of the innumerable unnamed tributaries of McKinney Creek, then double-back northeast to follow the powerline slash all the way to the Mount Baldy ski road. Ford McKinney Creek and soon you will be on the road. Turn right for the remains of Camp McKinney.

It is very easy to go off route into the maze of little logging roads that cover the McKinney Creek watershed. If you find yourself driving more south than east, you are probably off the trail, but don't worry. Keep going, taking major left turns to keep as high on the hillside as possible and you should emerge, after crossing McKinney and Rice Creeks, on the Baldy Road below Camp McKinney. Turn left and the town is eight miles north.

Disastrous forest fires in 1919 and 1931 virtually annihilated the old swashbuckling gold town but enough remains to hint of past glory. A few derelict mine buildings stand beside the road and hidden in the forest opposite are a few crumbling cabins, one a very high and narrow two-storey structure. The church is gone, the stores are gone, the saloons are gone. Even the workmen's shacks are burned or have rotted away. But you can walk a length of the old main street north of the new road and if you searched carefully you might find the old graveyard. Nothing beside remains — except of course for the tantalizing thought of those two gold bricks hidden somewhere along the way. You didn't find them, did you?

Up and Down the Gentle Granby

One of the loveliest of British Columbia's rivers must surely be the Granby, which flows into the Kettle at the little city of Grand Forks. It flows lazily in great sinuous loops, fragmenting into sandbars and islets, changing its color through a spectrum of greens and blues and browns as it weaves in and out of the sunlight, from deep pools to sandy shallows. Over the centuries the river has hollowed out a wide, flat-bottomed valley — a surprise among the mountainous forests of boundary country — where farmers have put the rich river soil to good use.

Backroads that follow a river inherit something of the earth's rhythms; subject to the river's whims, they turn where it turns, flood when it floods and listen always to the music of its flowing waters. Backroads follow the Granby, on both sides of the river, for more than 20 miles. They, like the river, are slow and lazy miles, contented miles. What better choice for an afternoon drive?

The backroad begins and ends in Grand Forks, a city whose history is overshadowed by that of Phoenix, a glittering mining camp that flourished and faded, then rose again from the ashes of the 1919 copper slump. Phoenix, on its high perch on Spion Kop, had the glamor and the glory, the riches from Knob Hill, Montezuma, Old Ironsides and other fabulous

Left: Abandoned Doukhobor settlement beside July Creek, just west of Grand Forks. Above: Black slag heaps mark the site of the Grand Forks smelter beside the Granby River.

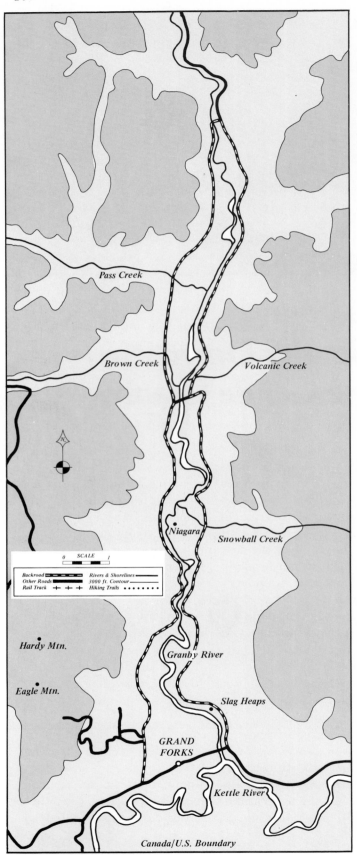

Pass Creek

Brown Creek

Volcanic Creek

SCALE

0   1

Backroad ▭▭▭▭   Rivers & Shorelines ▬▬▬
Other Roads ▬▬▬   3000 ft. Contour ▬▬▬
Rail Track ┼┼┼┼┼   Hiking Trails ••••••••

Niagara

Snowball Creek

Hardy Mtn.

Eagle Mtn.

Granby River

Slag Heaps

GRAND FORKS

Kettle River

Canada/U.S. Boundary

mines first worked in the 1890s. Grand Forks, 3,000 feet below Phoenix, shared the fate of Greenwood on the western side of the mountains. Both were minions. Here the dirty work of Phoenix the Splendid was done. Giant smelters in the valley processed Phoenix ores and left great piles of refuse, dark pyramids of slag that give the gentle Kettle Valley even today a stark and ominous air. Mining around old Phoenix has changed to an automated open-pit operation, its ore trucked down the mountain for processing in the Orient. Grand Forks, its ugly smelter long since dismantled has regained its pastoral air, a slow-paced country town more famous today for potatoes than copper.

In the city, one of the stateliest of Victorian mansions in the Interior dates from the glorious days of copper. Golden Heights, a turreted surprise on a bench above the highway, was built in 1891 by dentist "Doc" Averill, who, with his partner John Manley had previously completed Grand Forks' magnificent Yale Hotel. The house, with its towers and cupolas, bow windows and verandahs, has been restored and furnished by its present owners and is open to the public. The Yale Hotel, still in operation though not in the original building, serves good Russian food.

In the early days of exploration, when Grand Forks was known as Grand Prairie, the Granby River was called the North Fork of the Kettle. Its valley, which averages some 1,500 yards in width, with rich bottomland and natural meadows, attracted settlers. When Peter Verigin led his Doukhobor people west from the Prairies, Grand Forks' farmland tempted them to stay. They homesteaded on the north slope of the Kettle and up the west side of the Granby River, and their farms, sturdy pink two-storey houses with clusters of barns, are a distinctive feature of the landscape. The Granby Valley, though primarily agricultural, was not untouched by the mining boom. In 1906, gold and silver ores were found and mined at Franklin Camp, 45 miles upstream, and at Union Camp, five miles further. These operations lasted on, and off, for more than 40 years. A fluorospar deposit near Lynch Creek (the Rock Candy mine) was rich and important enough to warrant a twice weekly train service along a special spur of the Kettle Valley Railway. A wagon road was cut through to Franklin and the mines beyond. And at the Granby mouth, there was the smelter.

The backroad along the Granby begins at the eastern edge of Grand Forks where the highway crosses the Granby River bridge. Turn north beyond the bridge and head upriver. Almost at once you will reach the site of the Grand Forks smelter, built in 1809 with two furnaces that quickly expanded to eight. At that time it was the largest non-ferrous smelter in the British Empire, the third largest in the world, with a capacity of nearly 5,000 tons a day. When the Phoenix mines closed in 1919, the smelter shut down, was dismantled and moved to another mine site. The mountains of slag were left behind. Twenty years of tailings have been levelled into huge black shoulders above the river. Two final peaks, black and glittering like jet, are the smelter's only memorial. In one way, these slag heaps are an eyesore, but after 70 years or so they seem to belong to the valley, where they add an element of stark surprise to a landscape that is reminiscent of dry belt country. Chokecherries, elderberry, poison ivy and trails of wild clematis jungle the hillsides.

Soon after the road leaves the smelter site, rock bluffs pinch the valley together in a tight bottleneck, with the river in a canyon below. In the middle of the river is a tiny island, shaped like a steamboat, cribbed around with logs and crowned with a clump of cottonwood. This, and the abutments on the shore, are all that is left of the railway bridge which brought the trains of the Great Northern line up to the smelter. The road swings around the shoulder of the hill and the valley broadens, with the river running in sandy loops through the meadows. From now on, it's farm country, dotted with barns and homesteads, cows and hayfields, a pleasant river drive, sometimes right beside the water, sometimes a field or more away. And what a river! Crystal clear and languorous, with a sandy bottom. You could spend hours just watching and listening, absorbing the peace of the countryside, or fishing for rainbows and whitefish.

About 10 miles upstream, the road makes a sharp elbow bend to cross the river; if you are running short of time, you can start back to Grand Forks here. Otherwise, continue north along the road that slips between the river and a steep hillside and out into river meadows for another 10 miles of gentle driving before the second bridge. This is the end of the circuit, although the road continues to the site of Franklin Camp some 15 miles further, a good trip if you have the time. The return route down the west side of the river runs through country with much more settlement; in a way it is more interesting, with barns and well-kept log cabins, fields of barley, cows, horses, vegetable gardens and other signs of rural domesticity. In one of the bends of the river — still marked on provincial government maps — was the City of Niagara, founded in the days of the mining boom. Lots were put on the market and three or four saloons were open for business. Today the city has vanished without trace.

The Canadian Pacific Railway swings around this end of the Granby Valley on its way from Grand Forks to Greenwood, following contours some 600 feet above the road, around Thimble Mountain and up Brown Creek to Eholt. As the road nears Grand Forks, the railway creeps closer but it is not really apparent until the level crossing at the edge of town. The slopes of Eagle and Hardy Mountains were settled by Doukhobors in the early 1900s. One of the farmhouses, Mountain View, has been turned into a museum. Built in 1912 and occupied for 52 years, the farmhouse has been restored and furnished to present an accurate picture of early Doukhobor life. The kitchen and workshops are particularly interesting. You'll find the museum at the end of Hardy Mountain Road, a right turn off the road that brings you out on Highway 3 just west of Grand Forks.

Granby River valley is quiet, pastoral, with farms and barns and hayfields. Below: Old powerhouse of the Grand Forks smelter and the deep blue and green fishing pools of the river.

TOUR 18

The Cariboo River Trail

Cariboo. After more than 100 years, the word still stirs excitement in the blood. The fabulous days of the Gold Rush have long since faded but the romance lives on in the landscape, where the ranches and log settlements still seem to belong to another era, slower than our own. And scenically, if you know where to go, there's not another part of the province that can match its rich variety, its far-reaching horizons.

The oldest and most beautiful stretches of Cariboo country lie not beside the highway but along the little ranch roads that meander, with no apparent motives, through open parklands of pine and juniper, voluptuous meadows freckled with reedy lakes and clumps of birches, and westwards onto the great furrowed ridges of the Fraser trench. Here, the river coils through the hills like a thick, brown rope, puckering the benchlands into a maze of wrinkled valleys, incredibly complex, dry, silent, empty. The ranch roads twist and dip and double back on themselves, tracing delicate lines like snail trails across the hummocky hills.

There are several backroads through the Cariboo but perhaps the best of all is the 140-mile route from Lillooet to Williams Lake, a slower but more scenic alternative to Highway 97. It's a lonely road; the settlements along the way are few and so small and scattered that you could easily pass them by. It's a narrow road, a crooked road, a dusty road, but one that lingers in your memory when highway miles are long forgotten. The road is also a historic one, following the River Trail of 1859, the earliest route to the Cariboo goldfields. The wagon road, which started from Lillooet shortly afterwards, took initially the same route, then veered away from the river to Clinton and followed the forested eastern ridges of the plateau to meet the river again at Soda Creek.

From Lillooet, Mile 0 on the first Cariboo Road, follow Highway 12 for 22 twisting, climbing miles to Pavilion, then drive up to the junction at the Indian church a mile above. Turn left here, at the site of 22-Mile House, and follow the wagon road route up Pavilion Mountain, a steep, 3-mile switchback road that lifts you quickly through timber to a grass-covered plateau, some 4,000 feet above the Fraser. On this 10 square miles of unexpected tableland is the old Carson Ranch, now part of the huge Diamond S operations. Robert Carson, a Scot by birth who had emigrated with his family to Ohio, joined a wagon train to Oregon in 1858 when he was just 19. Lone survivor of an Indian massacre, he came north to try his luck in the Gold Rush. But as soon as he saw this land, so high and luxuriant with bunchgrass, he settled here, built a small log cabin and took up ranching, supplying hay and pigs to settlements along the way to the mines.

For years, stagecoaches and freight wagons toiled up Pavilion Mountain on their way to Barkerville by way of Cut-Off Valley and Clinton. Last staging post before the summit was 29-Mile House, now vanished, which stood at the fringe of the forest which clothes the upper plateau. Nearly 10 miles from the Indian church, the road finally reaches the summit (Pavilion forestry

*Above: Early morning
shadows at Clinton graveyard.
Opposite page: Originally
Haller's, then the OK Ranch,
this old timer straddles Big
Bar Creek north of Jesmond,
Right, traditional Russell
fence beside the road.*

lookout lies along a branch road to the left), then starts the steep zig-zag route down again, dropping almost 2,000 feet in less than four miles and providing a bird's eye view of Pear Lake, snuggled in the forested valley far below. Pavilion Mountain uplands are snowed in until late spring, and are sometimes impassable even in the middle of May. Before you try this route, check the condition of the road in Lillooet.

At the bottom of the hill, turn left for the fishing resort on Pear Lake, right for Kelly Lake and the Cariboo. Kelly Lake, which the road skirts, was named for settler Edward Kelly who ranched here in 1866. The water is clear and very cold and there is good fishing for rainbows. Beyond the lake, the road branches again, the main arm leading northeast through Cut-Off Valley to Clinton. This was the wagon road route, and it is also the route of the B.C. Railway which curves around the mountain from Pavilion. The River Trail, signposted to Jesmond, turns left up Porcupine Creek, following a narrow valley separated from the Fraser by the forested bluffs of Edge Hills, and hemmed in from the east by the colored limestone cliffs of the Marble Range. It's 20 miles to Jesmond through the woods, following the cleared swath of the Peace River powerlines. Jesmond was originally Mountain House, the name Phil Grinder gave the ranch that he established here in 1870. In 1919, when Henry Coldwell opened a post office in the ranch store, the government wanted a more distinctive name for the settlement. Coldwell chose Jesmond, the name of his English birthplace. A signpost at the junction beyond Jesmond directs you down to the Fraser at Big Bar, where there's excellent rock hunting on the sand bars that miners once worked for gold. The reaction ferry here has been in service since 1894, though the roads on the west bank are rough and lead only into the bush.

Four miles beyond Jesmond, where Big Bar Creek crosses the road, Joseph Haller, one of a group of Pennsylvania Dutch settlers, built his homestead. Known for years simply as "Haller's", it later became the famous OK Ranch, whose cluster of weathered, green-roofed buildings still stand in the curve of the road. The stones beside the creek in the ranch meadows are daubed with vivid red lichens and swallows swoop over the water. By now the forests have retreated, leaving dry rangeland hills interrupted only occasionally by stands of birch and pine and shallow lakes, alive with waterbirds and marshy with the industry of beavers. Further along, roads tempt you eastwards into the valleys of Big Bar and Meadow Lake and lead through to Highway 97 north of Clinton, good alternatives to the Jesmond-Pavilion Mountain section, particularly in the early snow-bound months. Other rougher roads lead through China Gulch and Crow's Bar to the steep canyon lip of the Fraser, which the River Trail avoided. Keep left at both the Big Bar Lake and the Meadow Lake junctions and continue through lovely Indian Meadows into Canoe Creek canyon, boxed in by a limestone wall of grey and ochre and red, fretted with little caves and pinnacles. Two sod-roofed log cabins stand derelict in the meadows.

Canoe Creek Indian village lies 10 miles past Meadow Lake junction and immediately beyond, beside a sea of brilliant green irrigated hayfields, is the two storey yellow frame ranchhouse of the B.C. Cattle Co. It's here that the River Trail finally begins its descent to the river, and presents that first, fine, lonely view of the Cariboo sky country with the river coiling peacefully through an endless wilderness of wrinkled brown hills. The colors are sombre; only a tuft of flowering rabbit-bush in August, the flame of a fall aspen, or an irrigated green patch of benchland brighten the landscape. The scale is immense; a car at the bottom of the hill is only a speck of color, a puff of dust; the road winding ahead only a scratch on the earth's hide.

For nearly 10 miles the road runs along the hilly benchlands of the Fraser, a circuitous route, through sandy sagebrush, past cliffs of wind-licked sand and volcanic contortions, in and out of steep dry gulches where stands of twisted pine provide little shade. Churn Creek (it is well named) churns into the Fraser from the west just south of the bridge leading to the great ranches of the Gang and Empire Valley. The Gang Ranch, so named because it was the first in the area to use the double-furrowed gang plough, was founded by the Harper brothers in 1883 and is the largest in area in North America. Keep right on the road that leads away from the river, climbs steeply up onto the dry plateau, then down again to the deep green hollow of Dog Creek, five miles away.

Dog Creek claims to be one of the oldest settlements in the Interior. A stopping place on the River Trail was built here in 1856. Dog Creek Hotel, as it was grandly called, advertised "the finest wines, liquors and cigars", provided stabling for 25 horses and was the head-quarters for the Dog Creek stage line, the first to be officially licensed in B.C. It still runs twice a week to Williams Lake, but the stagecoaches of old have been replaced by sturdy blue buses. Dog Creek also had the first flour mill on the mainland (built in 1866) and a water-driven sawmill owned by the Count of Versepeuch from France who built a substantial house and traded his elegant court clothes — his tri-cornered hat and blue satin jacket — with Indian Chief Alexis for a string of horses. Indians lived at Dog Creek long before the Europeans came: in a huge cavern at the base of the basaltic escarpment above the village Indian youths used to pray, sleep and dance during their initiation. The back wall of the cave is decorated with pictographs.

Dog Creek general store and post office offers cool refreshments, a chance to buy some cowboy jeans or a hat, or to fill your car with gas. The two-storey log building is about 10 years old, built from the logs of a far older structure. A road runs up the creek past the ranch and back to Meadow Lake road for access to Highway 97. But the River Trail keeps straight, winding around the creek and up onto the arid bench-lands again, where in summer, among the sagebrush, you can find numbers of Mariposa lilies like silky, three-petalled tulips of a delicate pale purple. The derelict ruins of Captain

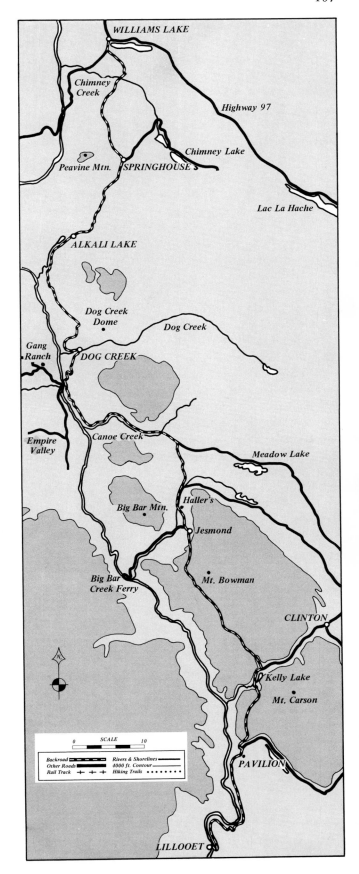

Above: The Fraser near Dog Creek, coiling through the ageless, wrinkled hills like a thick brown rope. Sunflowers spread a golden carpet on forested river benches.

Opposite page: Vanished landmarks of the Cariboo wagon road north of Lillooet, photographed in 1972. Top: Red roof barns of Alkali Lake Ranch, one of the oldest in B.C.

William Meason's ranch stands gaunt on a canyon lip beside the road. The big house burned down; only a couple of cabins and a corral are left of the ranch, founded in 1879 and stretching for eight miles along the river benches.

As the road climbs higher away from the river, the pines return to soften the landscape and in spring, the gold of sunflowers shines beneath the trees. Alkali Lake, 22 miles from Dog Creek, lies in an irrigated valley, an excellent spot for birds. Here you might see one of B.C.'s small colony of white pelicans which nest only at Stum Lake north of the Bella Coola road and come this way on migration. Bullock's orioles, bobolinks and long-billed curlews are three other splendid birds to watch for here.

Alkali Lake Ranch a mile beyond the lake is a photogenic arrangement of squared log barns with brilliant red roofs. The general store has a post office — and a hitching post. The ranch was started in 1861 on the site of an old roadhouse and claims to be the oldest cattle ranch in the province. The Indian village of the same name sits on a bench to the right of the road, its line of log houses punctuated by a white church. Beyond the village, the country becomes more domestic; the meadows are smaller, greener, and there are more trees. As you pass through the scattered community of Springhouse 13 miles further, you can't fail to notice one of the best stretches of Russell fence in the Cariboo. Along both sides of the curving road, the fence is one of the landmarks of Cariboo country, along with the better known snake fence. The Russell fence has five rails supported by tepee arrangements of poles instead of uprights, the whole being strung together with wire. It looks insubstantial, as if the first breath of wind would bring about its collapse; but it's sturdy — it will last for decades — and easy to build. What a pity that barbed wire is taking its place!

At Springhouse you realize, as the countryside closes in with pines, that you are leaving the open Fraser country and heading for civilization. There's a last sprinkle of lakes, Boitano and Westwick, backed by grassy meadows, and then it's forest the rest of the 19 miles to Williams Lake, where the River Trail joins the Cariboo Wagon Road.

On the Quiet Side of the Thompson

The Trans-Canada Highway, that most purposeful and time-saving of all the travel routes through British Columbia, follows the south bank of the Thompson River from Kamloops 40 miles to Chase. It's a good road, but a busy one, permitting few opportunities to stop and enjoy the countryside. But on the far side of the river, along a road that covers the same basic mileage and direction, you can loiter all you like, and this, after all, is what backroads are for.

To find this quiet route, take the Yellowhead Highway (Highway No. 5) north from the city across the river. Here sits the Kamloops Indian residential school, a huge red brick building opened in 1889. Beyond the school, where the highway starts a sharp left hand curve, a gravel road cuts right, down to the river bank. At once, you're into the silent sagebrush, dry and dusty in summer, with the river surging beside you and the noise of the highway on the opposite shore only a muffled roar. There's time to linger now, to watch the summer flycatchers in the cottonwood trees or photograph the milkweed pods beside the road. Travellers on the highway south of the river see from afar the great eroded clay banks that mark some ancient, higher water level. In fall, with mists smoking off the river, the pale line of pinnacled cliffs seems far away and unapproachable. On the backroad, however, you can drive right under them, admiring their fantastic castle shapes, fretted by wind and rain and slashed into gulleys by streams. Between the cliffs and the river lie long fields of hay and alfalfa, pungent in places with sharp yellow clouds of wild mustard. Where irrigation stops, sagebrush and desert weeds return. The contrasts are exhilarating.

About five miles along the road, when you have passed the most spectacular of the cliffs, a side road threads left through a draw to the Harper Ranch, founded in 1862, one of the earliest in the Kamloops area. Jerome Harper came to B.C. in 1859 from Virginia by way of California. His brother, Thaddeus, joined him and together they founded a cattle empire on more than 4,000 acres. When local ranchers sent their beef on the hoof to feed the hungry gold camps of the Cariboo, it was at Harper's that the cattle were marshalled for the long drive north. In 1889 the ranch was bought by Western Ranching Co. which three years later damned Paul Creek to form a storage lake for irrigation. Today, there's a government campsite on Paul Lake, and good fishing for rainbow trout. The Harpers went on to found the famous Gang Ranch in the Chilcotin.

The side road drives right up to the ranch house door and through the yard past a fine log house — the dogs will come barking; then it splits around the bulge of Harper Mountain, the left fork ploughing through rich meadows to Schiedam Lake and the Paul Lake road, the right cutting across to Pinantan Lake, some eight miles further. But don't go fishing yet. After a look at the ranch, return to the river.

This backroad is surprisingly well signposted; the road to the ranch is marked "Harper Road" and the road along the river is called "Shuswap Road" because it leads ultimately to Little Shuswap

Left and Above: Sand castles and sagebrush on the quiet north side of the Thompson River.

Above: Towards Chase the countryside becomes less arid, changing to green meadows with old homesteads.

Lake. A cement works on the river bank some miles further on strikes a discordant note in an otherwise harmonious landscape. There's a bridge back over the Thompson here, if you really have to return to the highway hubbub. Some 20 miles beyond the start of the road, the cliffs that have been hemming in the river's northern shore fall back a little and the road turns north through a rocky draw under the shadow of a cliff formation known as the Lion's Head. Here, the country is arid sagebrush scrub and pine. But watch carefully: somewhere within the next 10 miles the Interior Dry Belt will merge with the Interior Wet Belt and by the time you reach Chase, all the sagebrush will be gone. Through the draw, the road angles right and continues through dry pine woods high above the river flatlands which are now broader and more pastoral. Ignore a left signpost to Hyas and Pinantan Lakes unless you have time for a diversionary fishing expedition and keep going for about six miles past Lion's Head towards Whiskers Hill. Here a road sidles right down a most inviting gap towards broad green fields and a narrow wooden bridge which crosses the river to Pritchard. Walter Pritchard, a driver for the Okanagan Stage, settled here in 1912 and built a store and a hotel. A store still operates.

Resist the temptation to go to Pritchard and follow the signposted road to McGillivray Lake, which keeps high above the river, cutting a ledge around a rock bluff which provides a fine view over the river to the opposite forested shore. The McGillivray Lake road branches left five miles beyond the Pritchard turning. The lake is 20 miles north and offers rainbows to 2 lbs, boats and accommodation. This road links up with Tod Mountain ski resort and roads west to the Yellowhead Highway north of Kamloops. Keep right at the junction. A mile or so beyond, past an abandoned orchard, there are Indian pictographs around the entrance to two small caves on the hillside to the north. It's a short climb up the grassy hill to the granite cliff where the caves are, but the paintings of deer, eagle, bear tracks and other symbols, plus the view, make the effort worthwhile. In John Corner's book *Pictographs of the B.C. Interior,* this is known as the Niskonlith Site, for on the other side of the hill is long Niskonlith Lake. In spring, the flowers are massed in blue and gold, avalanche lilies, balsam root sunflowers and lupins and it's also the best time for trout fishing.

As the road nears Chase and Little Shuswap Lake, the country, which is wetter now, shows signs of settlement — and abandonment. Old orchards and homesteads, barns with fretwork roofs, corrals and broken fences stand in picturesque decay. In fall, with the aspens lit up and the grasses tawny, the area's deserted beauty is most appealing. Just before the lake, an Indian village groups its buildings around a church, then the road bends to cross the river to the little town of Chase. William Wingfield Chase started a ranch here in 1862 while working part time as a packer and a lumberman for the Hudson's Bay Co. at Kamloops. In 1908, Adams River Lumber Co. built a company town here, naming it after the first rancher. Today, it's a pleasant little town, its main street thankfully bypassed by the highway.

If you make this trip in October, don't leave the area without driving further east to see the sockeye salmon spawning in the Adams River. The Adams is only a short river, a meandering stream not three miles long from Adams Lake to Shuswap Lake but it's the richest salmon spawning stream in the world. In October, particularly in a cycle year, the river runs red as a million and a half salmon thrash in the shallows. The miracle of the salmon at the end of a quiet backroad will complete the day. Drive east along the Trans-Canada Highway until you reach Squilax where an overpass will take you beside the Adams River.

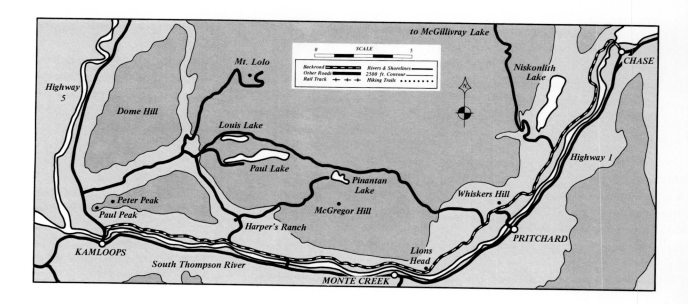

TOUR 20

Through Upper Hat to Ashcroft

At the road forks by the Indian settlement of Pavilion on a high and arid bench above the Fraser River, travellers must make a choice: to follow the first Gold Rush trail over Pavilion Mountain to the Cariboo or to loop eastwards, slipping through Marble Canyon with its limestone cliffs and string of pretty little lakes. Pavilion Mountain road, which climbs to more than 4,000 feet, hoards its snow late into the spring and is the less travelled route (see Backroad No. 18). Through Marble Canyon, Highway 12 cuts the shortest road from Lillooet to Cache Creek. But halfway along, a forgotten backroad branches south to follow Hat and Oregon Jack Creeks to the sagebrush benches of the Thompson River below Ashcroft. It would be difficult to find a more varied route than this. The dizzying verticality of Fraser country, canyons, lakes, wide open ranchlands, alpine meadows, forest and sagebrush — this 40 mile backcountry route tastes them all.

Pavilion is an old Indian settlement. Long before Europeans came this way, it was the Salish custom to bury their dead by placing them at the foot of a rock slide, then disturbing the rocks above so that a new slide covered the bodies. The position of the "grave" was marked by a pole, sometimes with a rag or streamer tied to the top. French-Canadian fur traders called them flags — in French "pavillons". There was a prominent "pavillon" here when the first white explorers came through in the 1880s. The name, though anglicized, has remained. Pavilion today is a two-part village; one part clusters around the station of the B.C. Railway while the other strings out along a bench about a mile up the road. At the lower village stands Pavilion Lodge, with an old sign still advertising "Rooms to Let", although today it is a store, one of those rare and fascinating places, a post office and country general store that keeps its musty cluttered air even though its main provisions are modern convenience foods. On hot days — and the Fraser Canyon heat is fierce — you can buy cold pop and ice-cream and cool off in the shade on the old front porch which has seen a lot of summers, a lot of swallows nesting in the eaves. There's a gas station here too, the only one between Lillooet and Cache Creek.

At the upper village, the road forks, the Indian trail coming in from the east meeting the Gold Rush Trail over the mountain. Here, on the site of 22-Mile House, where extra horses were kept for the long haul up to the Carson Ranch on the summit, stands a straggling line of Indian houses and a neglected church, its decorative turret crimped like a pie crust. Turn right at the forks. The road follows the northern rim of the valley carved out by Pavilion Creek as it washes down from the lake to join the Fraser. Like all flat areas in this vertical land, the valley is planted with rye and alfalfa and gives, with irrigation, two crops of hay a year. The green of the fields in spring is vivid against the darker mountains.

Four miles from Pavilion church is Pavilion Lake, long and irregular, that fills the canyon floor, and leaves only a little room on the north side for the road and a few resort cabins, and no room at

*Lichens and bleached bones
beside the Upper Hat
Creek road. Below: Cornwall
Lookout, forest service
eyrie above Ashcroft.*

Above: The old Parke Ranch with its green-roofed house and assortment of rail fences and corrals. Left: Mineral lake once mined for Epsom Salts near Venables Valley south of Ashcroft.

all on the south, where the cliffs fall steeply into the water. It's a cold, clear lake of varying colors and the promise of good fishing (rainbows to 3 lbs.). On the north side of the lake tower the marble cliffs that give the canyon its name, though the rock is not marble at all, but limestone of sunny bronze and cream colors in towers and pinnacles and one astounding pillar pointing skywards. About halfway down the lake, look for a sign pointing to Indian pictographs. The canyon was an important Indian trade route and two known pictograph sites are here. The first, because of its nearness to the road, is one of the best known in the province and is marked with a government plaque. The second, 3.4 miles further east, is a half-mile north of the road. Follow a trail up a steep gulley to a wall of smooth, cream-colored rock, a natural canvas for Indian paintings. Here you can trace in faded red the figures of bighorn sheep (once numerous in the area), bear tracks, men with bows and arrows and other symbols.

The eastern end of Pavilion Lake and two other lakes in the chain, Turquoise and Crown, are in Marble Canyon Provincial Park. The government campsite beside a beach on Crown Lake is a popular spot. Turn right at the sign to Hat Creek, about 5½ miles from the campsite, onto a road which winds beside the creek into a thicket of aspen and cottonwood. At a bend in the road an irrigation flume arches high overhead. Take the left branches at the next two forks and continue almost due south through Hat Creek valley. The creek, which flows into the Bonaparte River north of Cache Creek, was given its original name, Riviere aux Chapeaux (River of Hats), because of a rock near its mouth that was pitted with hat-shaped cavities. Hat Creek valley is mostly open range country, dotted with stands of aspen and pine — a little bit of the Cariboo. It's a country to linger in, to notice the colors and textures of the countryside: vivid orange lichens on boulders; sunflowers in spring and rabbit bush in August; the strange colors of the alkaline lakes that dimple the hills; a multitude of horned larks running beside the road and kestrels perched, it seems, on every roadside pole; the smell of sage, dry and pungent; the dark forests of the distant hills. Rock hounds will like the valley: there are deposits of petrified wood about 3½ miles down the road and at the divide between Hat and Oregon Jack Creeks, while on the ridge northeast of Upper Hat Creek settlement are outcrops of jasper and agate.

Upper Hat Creek, 12 miles from the turnoff, used to have a post office, but today the settlement looks, to uninitiated eyes, merely a ranch. Further along, the old Parke ranch sits among neat hayfields, a cluster of barns and corrals around the twin-gabled house with its soft green roof. Beyond the ranch, the road swings sharply left (east) to skirt a marshy meadow area then dives through a stand of young birches that in fall spread a carpet of gold along the road. Langley Lake, sludgy edged and used as a cattle watering hole, comes into view as the valley narrows. Steep cliffs of red and orange rear up beside the road to the north, and soon afterwards, the road becomes a forest road, cool and green, running beside Oregon Jack Creek.

Four miles past the lake, a road branches left up Three Sisters Creek to Cornwall Forestry Lookout. The road is good, climbing steeply but safely through thinning forests and up above the timberline into alpine meadows. The lookout station on the 6,684-foot summit, pops into view five miles along, a little white box on stilts on a rounded rock bluff. Visitors are welcome to go in and see the view from the tower — on fine days you can see back to Mount Baker, east to the Rockies and north to Mount Waddington — and to learn something of the important work of the fire-watchers. Spring comes late at this elevation: the alpine meadows are not usually in bloom until the middle of July.

Returning down the hill and through the forests along Oregon Jack Creek, it's seven miles to the sagebrush with wide open, hazy vistas of the Thompson, as the road emerges on open slopes above Highway 1, just opposite a fruit stand. Ashcroft Manor, six miles north up the highway, is a worthy destination point, a roadhouse on the Cariboo Wagon Road since 1862 and still in service as a motel. The Cornwall brothers (the mountain was named after them) came to Canada from Ashcroft in Gloucestershire, England to join the gold rush. But after a visit to the mines, they chose ranching instead. One long look at the deep sea of bunchgrass that waved on the Thompson flats

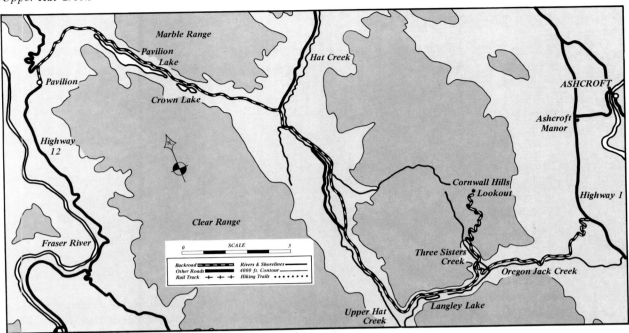

convinced them that here lay a future more certain than gold. The brothers pre-empted a thousand acres in 1859, built a small cabin and fetched in cattle from Coeur D'Alene. In 1862, the new wagon road from Yale to Barkerville passed nearby so they built a stopping house beside the road, and named it after their English home. The original structure, though since enlarged and modified, can still be seen. Ashcroft Manor supplied the Cariboo mining camps with beef; later a water-driven sawmill was built and then a flour mill, using stones hauled up from Esquimalt. The Cornwall brothers married and settled down to make Ashcroft as much like "home" as possible. They built a diminutive Anglican church with a steeple and eight hand-hewn pews; they had English nannies for their children, afternoon teas and garden parties and even fox hunts. Over the sagebrush and prickly pear, over the waving bunchgrass went the Ashcroft hunt, complete with pink jackets and hunting horns and all the traditions. The fact that there were no foxes didn't bother them one bit. There were coyotes instead.

When the CPR drove through the Thompson Valley in the 1880s, a station was built at Ashcroft down by the river, and with this new transportation route to the coast, the wagon road declined. The settlement and the trade moved down to Ashcroft station, now the town of Ashcroft. But the manor remains, a historical site, though unrestored and unsubsidized. Descendents of the Cornwalls live there still and cabins behind the manor are for rent. The family church sits intact on the Indian reserve beside the road leading down to Ashcroft.

In the hills southwest of Ashcroft are lakes so heavily alkaline that they were once "mined" for Epsom salts. To reach them, an interesting side trip, take the road that branches off Highway 1 six miles south of the junction with Upper Hat Creek Road. This begins as a narrow dirt road twisting beside a stream through a dense grove of trees, but it quickly climbs up into an open grass valley. The lakes lie a mile or so along the road, so choked with minerals that at first glance they seem to be frozen over, white and glittery and spotted (like Spotted Lake on Richter Pass west of Osoyoos). Back in the 1930s a commercial venture carried off the salts for processing. One of the lakes has various wooden constructions dating back to those days, though the buildings that used to stand in a meadow nearby are gone. If you continue on the road beyond the lakes you can circle back through Venables Valley to the highway near a Canadian National Railways' flag stop called, appropriately enough, Epsom. The backroads in this area are confusing, however, so be sure you have a good map.

TOUR 21

Wagon Road to Quesnel Forks

The road to Likely, 50 miles to the east of the Cariboo Highway, sees far fewer travellers now than 100 years ago, when miners by the thousands tramped its steep and dusty ways to the rich placer gold creeks of Keithley, Antler, Williams and Lightning. For this was the route of the first trail to the goldfields of Cariboo, started in 1859. The Cariboo Wagon Road, built six years later, took a different route beyond 158-Mile, swinging in to Barkerville from the west by way of Quesnel and Cottonwood, the same route followed today by the highway. When the wagon road was complete, the Goldfields Trail was gradually abandoned. Never subject to the harassment of highway travel, settlements along the Trail today have an older, quieter charm and the atmosphere of gold rush days is perhaps a little easier to recreate, particularly in such a place as Quesnel Forks, the best preserved of all B.C.'s ghost towns.

The landscape on the eastern rim of the Cariboo Plateau is very different from that of the Fraser River benchlands. The dry belt is left behind and you're into the parklands zone, which is densely covered with shady jackpine and spruce and stands of aspen. There are lakes a plenty, shimmering spots in the evergreens where waterbirds of many different sorts make their summer homes. How the first travellers must have hated the country — thick with mosquitoes and flies in summer, a mire in spring and fall, and covered in winter by incredible snowfalls; with steep mountains and wide, rushing rivers and trails so narrow and precipitous that often whole mule trains were lost. But they came, whatever the season, whatever the hazards, because in the creeks lay gold.

The Goldfields Trail leaves the Cariboo Highway at 150-Mile House, the former interchange point with stages for the Chilcotin. The wagon road was intended to run along the shore of Williams Lake but a bribe in the form of a loan from a local rancher persuaded the contractors to locate the road further east, bypassing the settlement of Williams Lake. For five miles further, the wagon road and the trail follow a common route. Two miles along, the new road cuts off a loop of the wagon road and along this gravel loop is 153-Mile Ranch. In the early years of the century, Italian immigrant Louis Crosina brought his family from nearby Mountain House to start a homestead here. He ended up by building a family settlement, with a store and trading post, a large two-storey log house, a blacksmith shop and several barns. His daughter, Alice Lillian, ran the store single handed until her death in 1963. All the buildings are now part of the Patenaude ranch and the store is closed, but it's still stocked with goods, just the way Miss Crosina left it. The Patenaude family looks after the store and hopes one day it will become a museum. If you plan to drive down this stretch of road to see the red and white log store, remember it is on private property and you should ask permission at the ranch before you stop to peer in through the windows to take a photograph.

Two miles beyond Crosina's, a road branches right to Miocene and Horsefly, which was first called Harper's Camp after the founders of the Gang Ranch, then renamed, along with a lake and a river, in honor of the flies that infest the area. It was on the Horsefly River in 1859 that Peter Dunlevy found the first gold in the Cariboo, though the richer creeks were further north. Today the settlement is a sportsman's centre, with big game hunting and fishing on the lake for 20-lb char. Keep left at the junction for the four-mile journey over Carpenter's Mountain to the site of 158-Mile or Mountain House, now vanished. Here the wagon route branches left to rejoin the Cariboo Highway by way of Deep Creek. Keep right for Likely and continue through unbroken spruce forest, cool and shady, for 15 miles to Big Lake Ranch, the monotony of the forest broken only by Skulow Lake with its fishing resort and fringe of trembling aspens. At Big Lake, the road breaks through into rolling meadowland, with old log fences, barns and cabins and a lovely white frame house with a verandah. Big Lake, true to its name, has one large lake and a scattering of smaller ones, Parker, Alpha, Peter and brighten, around the hump of Limestone Mountain.

From here, the road descends into the Beaver Valley, a string of lakes nestling in a green trough of water meadows, and makes a right-angled turn to cross Beaver Creek on a one-way bridge. Just before the bend, a road heads west to the Cariboo Highway at McLeese Lake, a long, straight, dull 19 miles. The log buildings at Beaver Lake are on the site of one of the most famous of the Cariboo stopping places, founded in 1861 by Peter Dunlevy with the proceeds of his mining. Dunlevy later sold out and went to Soda Creek where he built the sturdy log Colonial House and a Frenchman called Francois Guy took over. Soon it was called Guy's Place. A Cariboo miner, J.C. Bryant, praised Beaver Lake House in his journal of 1863 in these words: "The hotel is the best between Victoria and the Cariboo, indeed Victoria hotels could not compare with this one in the splendid meals given to the guests". He went on to describe a sumptuous dinner of baked meats, fresh vegetables, huge huckleberry pies and fresh cream. In addition to the inn, two stores were here, a gambling hall and some kind of an animal market. Today, a small cafe-cum-store still caters to the travellers.

A side road turns right to follow the meadows of the Beaver Valley over to Horsefly and the Likely road climbs fairly steeply up the hill beyond the lake to regain the 3,000-foot level of the forested tableland. Twelve miles along, still on the high plateau, is Morehead Lake, formed when the creek was dammed to provide the water supply for the huge hydraulic operations at the Bullion mine. The road runs along the top of the earth dam at the lake's western end, then descends to the settlement of Hydraulic by Little Lake. As its name suggests, Hydraulic owes its existence, too, to the Bullion mine on the south banks of the Quesnel River. Three miles beyond Hydraulic a side road leads left through the bush to the Bullion ghost town and the fantastic excavation in Dancing Bill's Gulch.

Thomas Latham, alias Dancing Bill, struck gold on the river late in 1859; a day's labor earned him an average of $75, but as soon as the gold appeared to be on the wane, he left in search of easier riches. Twenty years later, the claim was reworked by Chinese who dug into the benchlands and discovered the old river channel and $900,000 in gold. They cleaned up and went on their way. By the 1890s, most of the rich deposits had been taken from the Cariboo creeks. Gold remained plentiful, but it was scattered thinly in the gravel banks of the rivers. In 1892, J.B. Hobson interested a syndicate of Victoria businessmen in a scheme to crush the gravel from 2,500 acres of the old Quesnel River bed and extract the gold. The potential, he figured, was $100 million. The Cariboo Hydraulic Mining Co. was formed, later bought out by Consolidated, and the work began. For the operation. Hobson needed water, lots of it. He built 21 miles of ditches in 1897 to carry water down from Bootjack and Polley lakes and the following year he dammed Morehead Creek and built another canal to divert its water. The gravel banks were sluiced down with giant hoses and the sludge was filtered to recover the gold. Every year, Dancing Bill's Gulch became wider and deeper. Still more water was needed, however, and for this Hobson had to find new investment. Controlling shares were bought by New York interests and Hobson started on his $200,000 scheme to bring water down from Spanish Creek, 10 miles away. In 1906, with no word of explanation, the U.S.

Right: Quesnel Forks, the best preserved of B.C. ghost towns, sits in a grassy meadow in the arms of the Quesnel and Cariboo Rivers. Top: Crosina's store at 105-Mile, closed, but still wonderfully intact. Above: Dandelion seedheads whiten the fields of Beaver Valley edged by a typical Cariboo fence.

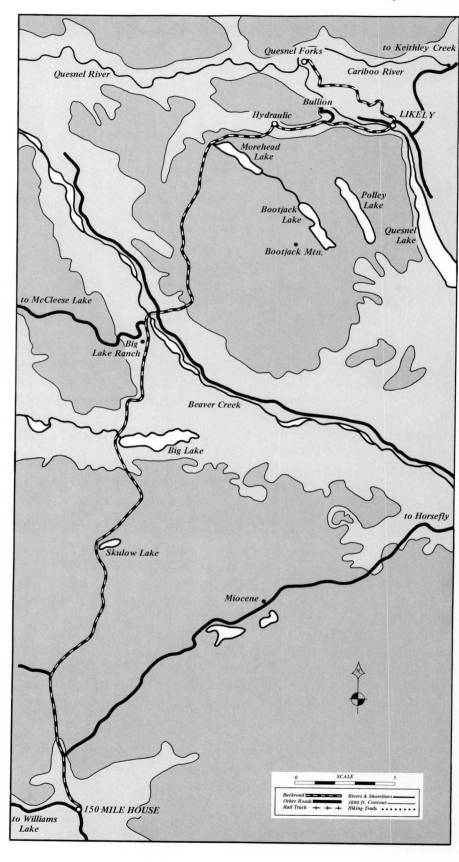

partners ordered all work on the Bullion abandoned. Hobson left his home on the lip of the gulch, and moved away, too disappointed to try again. He died soon afterwards.

The Bullion mine was reworked yet again in the 1930s by a Vancouver syndicate under Ray Sharpe. Using more water per day than the city of Vancouver, two million cubic yards of earth a year were removed from the gulch. And for every yard of earth, a quarter of an ounce of gold was gleaned. After 10 years, the gold was exhausted and Dancing Bill's Gulch was left a monstrous chasm, two miles long and 250 feet deep. Hobson's mansion still remains, a dark, tattered ghost in the meadows, and round about are other ruins, of bunkhouses and offices and sundry others. It's a desolate spot.

The road to Bullion was the original route of the Goldfields Trail which went across the river, first by ferry, then by toll bridge, to Quesnel Forks. But the bridge long ago was washed away. To reach Quesnel Forks today you first go to Likely, six miles from Hydraulic. This settlement on the river three miles downstream from Quesnel Lake, dates from the much later gold rush of the 1930s when a strike was made at Cedar Creek. Originally named Quesnel Dam, the village was renamed after John "Plato" Likely who worked claims in Likely Gulch and on Cedar Point. He earned his nickname because he was a great admirer of Plato and Socrates and would talk philosophy for hours with everyone he met. Today, a neat lodge, cafe, store, gas station and other tourist facilities are strung out along a green bench beside the river, headquarters for anglers and hunters.

Drive up the hill behind for half a mile, then turn left along a signposted road to Quesnel Forks. The eight miles of forested road are narrow and rough, climbing high through an ugly burned area, then dropping down to the river again. Quesnel Forks lies beautifully situated at the confluence of the Quesnel and the Cariboo rivers. The Cariboo was originally known as the North Fork of the Quesnel, so the settlement at the river forks was given an obvious name. It's the oldest of the Cariboo gold camps, founded in 1860 and for a short time it was the largest settlement on the B.C. mainland. In 1861, the Royal Engineers surveyed a proper townsite here, because it was realized that the town would be an important supply centre for all the gold creeks. On the 10-acre flat in the arms of the rivers were 20 houses, 12 stores, saloons, a jail, boarding houses, cabins, and a mining office. The Forks prospered for five years, but started its decline when the wagon road was built from Quesnel Mouth (now Quesnel) to Barkerville. The white miners soon abandoned the town, but the Chinese stayed on for years, carefully working the river bars.

Fifteen or so of the buildings of Quesnel Forks still remain on the quiet river bench; they were sturdily built of massive logs and will last longer yet, while the grass grows tall about them and river cottonwoods steal slowly back again. It's a beautiful place, with a melancholy sense of history. In the scattered graveyard east of the town only a few headstones remain, tangled in salmonberry bushes. But the river, which destroyed the bridge in a freshet of rage, periodically assaults the town itself. Already the jail and the express company buildings are gone and others near the shore are threatened. And the heavy snows of the bleak Cariboo winters constantly batter Quesnel Forks, the loveliest ghost town in B.C. It deserves protection.

Return to Likely the way you came. Drive north along the shore of the lake to the gold camp site of Cedar Creek, now a resort community, with a government campsite on Cedar Point. Or, if you have a sturdy car, you can turn left up Poquette Creek to join the Goldfield Trail again by the Cariboo River and follow it to Keithley Creek. This was one of the great names in Cariboo history, a rambunctious tent town of 10,000 in the heady 60s. Barkerville lies 25 miles beyond, over rough mountain roads susceptible to washouts and slides and suitable only for four-wheel drives. Go this way if you can, for what more satisfying destination can there be? Otherwise, you must return to the Cariboo Highway the way you came, and take the wagon road route to Barkerville.

TOUR 22

A Taste of the Chilcotin

Huge and lonely, with some of the highest mountains, wildest rivers, thickest forests and biggest cattle ranches in B.C., the Chilcotin has often been called more a state of mind than a geographic location. It is placed loosely between the Fraser River and the Coast mountains and is drained into the Fraser by the great Chilcotin River. Highway No. 20 meanders northwest through this sprawling country 300 miles to the sea at Bella Coola, a long, arduous, dusty trip that few travellers care to make, at least in both directions. But you can follow instead a much shorter loop road, barely 120 miles return from Williams Lake, which will provide a good taste of the Chilcotin country in all its splendid variety.

Fur traders were the first Europeans to see these forested hills. Fort Chilcotin, a trading post of the Hudson's Bay Co., was built near the confluence of the Chilko and Chilcotin rivers in 1828 and lasted for nearly 45 years. Then came men in search of gold, stalking all the tributaries of the Fraser. The Chilcotin, east of the river, was a disappointment, for all the gold lay in the Cariboo creeks. In 1862, civilization in the shape of a road threatened the isolated Chilcotin. Alfred Waddington began construction of a 16-foot-wide wagon road from the head of Bute Inlet as a fast route to the Cariboo goldfields. This invasion by the white man precipitated B.C.'s first and last Indian troubles in May 1864. A construction ferryman on one of the rivers along the route refused food to a couple of Chilcotin Indians. They killed him and returned to their camp to rally the rest of the tribe. That night, the main construction camp was attacked and 13 of the 16 men were killed. The site where this happened is now known as Tragedy Canyon. Further up the river, road boss George Brewster and his survey crew were also set upon, and three were killed. The construction men fled. The governor of the new colony, Frederick Seymour, and a crew of volunteers sailed north in HMS Sutlej to the head of Bentinck Arm; from there they hacked their way through the bush to Puntze Lake where they had arranged to meet reinforcements, a party of Cariboo miners led by gold commissioner George Cox. With the help of Chief Alexis, they tracked down eight suspects and took them to Quesnel. Five of them were later hanged.

Waddington's road was abandoned, but the trail that Governor Seymour slashed through from Bentinck Arm became the route of Highway 20, the Chilcotin Road. The loop tour of the Chilcotin follows this road west from Williams Lake for 33 miles. At first it's a fine paved highway, rising from the San Jose valley into the forests and clearings of the plateau, past Chimney Creek Ranch, then swooping down to cross the Fraser over the Sheep Creek Bridge. West of the river, after a 1,000-foot climb out of the river trench onto the plateau again, the pavement ends in a stretch of meadows with old log buildings typical of Chilcotin country. Past McIntyre Lake in its boulder-strewn fields the forests begin. Much of the Chilcotin Plateau is covered with forest, a dense shroud of jack pine and Douglas fir which provides summer range for the vast herds of cattle and much logging. Forestry has recently supplanted ranching as the chief factor in the area's economy.

At Riske Creek, 30 miles from Williams Lake, a forestry road branches left to Big Creek and Farwell Canyon, your return route. In the 1880s, when the first Chilcotin Road was finished as far as Hanceville (it went south of Bald Mountain; today's road, relocated in 1901, goes north) a post office was located at Becher House, the only saloon between 150-Mile and Hanceville. It provided meals for 25 cents, single beds for 35 cents and bottles of whisky for $1. The post office was called Chilcotin. Later the name was changed to honor the first settler, L.W. Riske, who founded the Cotton Ranch here in the 1870s and shipped ham, bacon and butter to Barkerville. Riske Creek today is still a ranching centre, a good base for fishing, hunting, rock-hounding and cross-country skiing. It has a white-painted log general store, a rodeo every June and the comfortable old Chilcotin Lodge keeps the name of the first post office alive.

From the meadows of Riske Creek the road climbs higher still, 23 miles through forests dappled with the bright green of meadows and the gleam of little lakes to the edge of the plateau where the road drops down onto benchlands of the Chilcotin River. On the escarpment, the B.C. government has put up a Stop of Interest sign commemorating Norman Lee's Yukon cattle drive. Lee came to B.C. in 1882, founded an Indian trading post at Redstone, then bought out Dan Norberg's cabin and store at Hanceville, which he called Beaver Ranch. His family live there still. The Klondike adventure, which made Lee famous throughout the Chilcotin must surely be one of the most epic journeys ever recorded. In 1898 he left Hanceville to drive 200 head of cattle to market — at Dawson City, 1,500 miles through the wilderness. The trip was a disaster: the cattle, emaciated from their long journey, were finally butchered and put on scows for the journey down the lake to Teslin, miles from their goal. The scows were wrecked, the beef was ruined and abandoned.

Hanceville was named for Tom Hance, who established a trading post in the area in the 1860s and later took up ranching. When the settlement had its first post office in 1889, Hance became postmaster. But Hanceville today is very much Norman Lee's town. "This is Lee's, B.C." is painted on a log barn beside the road and at the junction is Lee's Corner motel, store and cafe, open seven days a week. Hanceville post office is three miles down the road at a nearby ranch.

Turn left at Lee's junction and head south, winding through dry benches, bright in summer with oyster plants and blue flax flowers, to cross the Chilcotin River, a beautiful bright blue-green. Up the other side of the river trench, turn left again along the Fletcher Lake road, then right at the forks three miles beyond. Fifteen miles of good gravel road bring you through the forest to Fletcher Lake, a popular fishing resort area (rainbow to 3 lbs.) where a flat roadside meadow, gold in June with dandelions, provides good camping. Beyond the lake the road continues through marshes to two other small reedy lakes where yellow-headed blackbirds nest in the tules. To the south, is a fine distant view of the snowcapped mountains of the Coast Range.

Beyond the last lake is the settlement of Big Creek by the stream of the same name which the Indians called "Creek of Many Rabbits". Ahead lies Mons Lake, Big Creek post office and several guest ranches and resorts. Turn left along the forestry road that heads east across the plateau, wide and straight and monotonous, hemmed in by dark woods for nine miles until a meadow clearing and deserted homestead provide a welcome break. The old cabin has a sod roof and in the summer hundreds of swallows nest in the open rafters of the big log barn. Across the road, a shallow lake breeds mosquitoes for the swallows and the nighthawks, while red-winged blackbirds carol in the reeds. Thirteen more miles of forest bring you back again to the Chilcotin River at Farwell Canyon, one of the most spectacular in the province. The river, heavily laden with silt, has scoured a deep and sinuous trench through the sandy soil of the plateau. After the dark of the woods, the canyon is a surprise of sunny yellows and browns, a yawning chasm with pinnacles and towers, fretwork cliffs, caves and gulches, with the river a churning milky green far below. Shuswap Indians used to live here but the smallpox epidemic of 1862 killed them all. Their village sites on both sides of the river can hardly be distinguished but they left one tangible sign of their passing — pictographs are painted on an overhanging rock on a bench just south of the bridge.

The road corkscrews down to the river's edge to the one-lane wooden bridge, then zig-zags laboriously up again, out of the trench. The bridge is a new one. In 1964 the canyon wall collapsed, damming the river and drowning the old bridge. When the river finally burst through, the bridge was swept away. Its piers can still be seen downstream.

The Chilcotin is a beautiful river; its 125 miles from the Chilko to the Fraser are scheduled to be set aside as B.C.'s first "Wild River" park, a proposal that would also help to save the herd of California bighorn sheep that makes its home in the area. There are 400 sheep here in the reserve, perhaps one-fifth of the world's population. Watch out for them as you drive through the canyon and out onto the benches above.

Four miles from the bridge, you're finally on the plateau again, in undulating grasslands watered by Hargreaves Creek and a string of little unnamed lakes. On the right is the Indian settlement of Toosey in green meadows beside Riske Creek, and soon you're at Riske Creek itself, at the junction with Highway 20 for the return to Williams Lake.

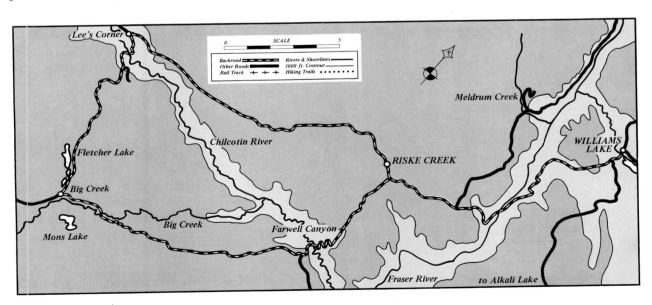

Top: Herding cattle in the lush green hills near Riske Creek. Above: Startled bighorn sheep bound to safety near the Chilcotin River, Right: The one-lane bridge over Farwell Canyon. Opposite Page: Canyon ranch tucked into a curve of the river, its meadow bright with wild mustard.

TOUR 23

By Deadman's Rippled Rocks

Deadman Valley pushes north from the Thompson River between Cache Creek and Savona, one of the hottest, driest and most barren stretches of country in the province. In the searing heat of summer, the name does little to encourage travellers, promising no relief from the desert and encouraging vague premonitions of disaster. Yet the road along the valley is a scenic one, passing rapidly from desert to green farmland and cooling off in the high forests of the plateau and a string of mountain lakes. Beside the river, which meanders in great sandy loops through the meadows, stand high volcanic cliffs, contorted and astoundingly fire-colored like the gates of Inferno. Here, you can search for agates and petrified wood or climb up to the hoodoos, five giant pillars of eroded rock that overlook the valley like sentinels.

The valley is essentially a deadend, unless you have a four-wheel drive vehicle and can thread your way through rough trails out to Highway No. 97 via Loon Lake. But there are approach roads from west and south so you don't have to retrace your steps all the way. The western road leaves the highway 1½ miles east of the village of Cache Creek on a gravel road which turns left into Pass Valley to meet Cache Creek in a wooded fringe of cottonwood. Except for the narrow strip of bush beside the creek this is still very much desert country. In summer, cactus, Opuntia fragilis, opens its great tissuey blossoms of yellow silk towards the sun and sagebrush fills the hot air with its spicey perfume. On eroded red volcanic cliffs above the road rattlesnakes bask on the ledges. They are in great numbers here, but will attack only if disturbed. If you brave the snakes, the cliffs are a good source of agate and natrolite, as rock hounds may know.

Tsotin Lake, a favorite with local anglers, lies about six miles along the road to the south, screened from view by trees. A side road gives access. The pine woods here are less arid, open and fragrant, with great tufts of blue-berried juniper, a few blue asters and brown-eyed susans in summer. Cache Creek wanders away to its birthplace in the rattlesnake hills and the road climbs over the pass, a mere 2,800 feet, and down to another lake with the unfortunate name of Stinking. If you go to the lake in early summer, when the water is high, you will wonder why it earned such a name. It's a beautiful spot, with a clearing at the western end for camping, a little shingle beach and many birds — a family of loons, spotted sandpipers, grebe, swallows, kingfishers, flickers and warblers. Further along is Cultus Lake (Cultus is the Chinook word for "Bad"), reed-rimmed and garrulous with "soldier" blackbirds. If you are lucky, you may even see some of the bats that live in a colony near the western end of the lake. They have been seen here flying in the daylight.

Charette Creek drains the marshes at the lake's eastern end. Back in the early days of the fur trade, a Mr. Charette, clerk of the North West Fur Trading Co. post at Kamloops, was found knifed to death at a camp beside an unnamed river. His murderer was never found, but the river became known first as Riviere des Defunts, then Knife River and then, during gold rush days, as Deadman's

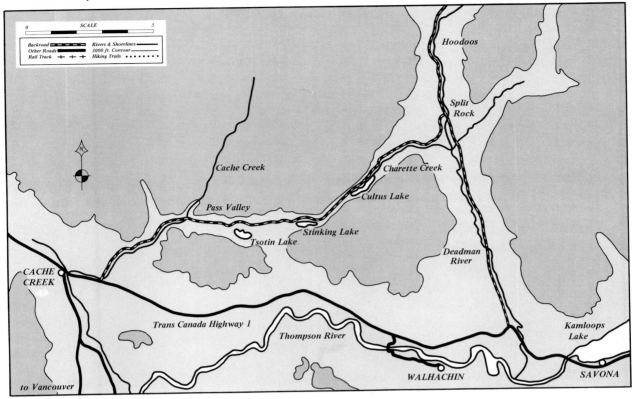

River. Charette Creek flows ultimately into the Deadman.

Four miles or so down the Charette, the road emerges from the woods onto a hillside, all sagebrush and desert scrub, and winds its way steeply down into Deadman Valley, with its lush meadows. As you round one of the turns you get the first breathtaking view of those fantastic cliffs, rumpled and rainbow-hued, rising a sheer 200 feet from the river. On the map, these are marked "Split Rock" and they are indeed fretted with caves and fissures and splits. Volcanic in origin, the cliffs provide good hunting for agates and petrified wood, and make a scenic backdrop for a picnic down by the river.

The most curious landmarks of the Deadman Valley are the five hoodoos, eroded pinnacles of rock and clay conglomerate, each topped by an overhanging capstone which protected the loosely-compacted rock underneath when the material around them washed away. To find the hoodoos, drive north up the valley from Split Rock to Deadman Creek Ranch and scan the cliffs east of the road. From a distance, the pillars look insignificant — it's easy to miss them entirely unless the light is right. Only close up can their immense size and sculptural beauty be appreciated. But before you start the hot and strenuous scramble up the hill, ask permission at the ranch. Cross the ranch bridge and head up a rounded hill of petrified yellow sand, then along a rocky slope. When you reach the hoodoos, their size will surprise you: they stand over 40 feet high and seem perilously unbalanced.

Along the valley you may have noticed an old irrigation flume clinging to the sides of the hills west of the river. In the early 1900s, a grandiose scheme was launched with American ingenuity (Charles Barnes) and British wealth (the Marquis of Anglesey) to reclaim the desert benches above the Thompson River and plant orchards. Water was led from Snohoosh Lake, further north up the Deadman Valley, along miles of wooden flume to irrigate the young orchards, which blossomed on the previously barren earth. A townsite called Walhachin (Indian for "abundant land") was built on the river's south bank and settlers flocked into the area. When the first crop of Jonathan apples was shipped to market in 1913, corn, tomatoes, onions, beans and tobacco had also been planted on the

benchlands, and it seemed as if the dream of Walhachin was coming true. Then came the First World War, and the young men of the town, all but ten, left for the battlefields of Europe. The orchards along the Thompson struggled on for a while without them, but the miles of flume and ditches needed constant checking and repair. Each year, spring freshets destroyed more of the irrigation system. The fruit trees languished from lack of water; the crops failed. And gradually the sagebrush crept back. The village of Walhachin remains, though shrunken now in size and splendor, and still a few gnarled relics of the apple orchards blossom hopefully each April on the sagebrush benches above the Thompson. Up the Deadman Valley, the irrigation flume, bleached bone-grey wood on the hillside, is an eloquent epitaph for broken dreams.

Above Deadman Creek Ranch, the valley narrows, the fields diminish and the desert hills turn into forest. About 10 miles from the ranch the road circles the east side of Mowich Lake, the first of four that thread the upper valley. Snohoosh Lake, the reservoir for Walhachin water, lies further north. The wooden cribbed dam at the outlet, built in 1910, was deliberately breached in later years to prevent its accidental collapse. Four miles further still is Skookum Lake, with its eroded tower of yellow sandstone, and waterlilies; then comes Deadman, then Vidette, probably the prettiest of the lakes in the valley. This lake, recently restocked with rainbow and kokanee trout, is a well-known fishing spot. Not so well known is its history of gold mining. In the 1930s mining engineers predicted that Vidette would become "one of the major gold producing areas in the province". The buildings at the lake's north eastern shore, now a ranch, are all that remains of those great expectations. A steep, rough road climbs right above the ranch onto the Kukwaus Plateau where, in July, the meadows are thick with wildflowers — Indian paintbrush, lupines, geraniums, asters and others. Six miles beyond Vidette Lake, the road divides after crossing Joe Ross Creek and the right branch leads a short distance down the Deadman River. You must park at the gate here and walk the short distance downstream to see the falls, 150 feet of hurtling white water in spring and early summer, and a beautiful three-strand cascade in fall that gives it the local name of Three Witches' Falls. This is the end of the trail for all but four-wheel drivers; return down to Vidette and along the lakes into the wide valley. But instead of turning up the hill at the Split Rock, continue south through the irrigated meadows, past the Indian village, and out to the Trans-Canada Highway west of Savona.

Opposite Page: Split Rock, fire-colored contortions above the green river meadows. Above: The five hoodoos of Deadman Valley, like craggy sentinels. Left: Petrified sand hills on hoodoos trail and rattlesnake rocks above Cache Creek.

TOUR 24

Ghosts of the Silver Slocan

T he Slocan is one of the most isolated regions of Southern British Columbia, a bony shoulder of land imprisoned by great mountain ranges and long meandering lakes which challenge highway construction. The nearest settlement of any size is the city of Nelson, miles to the south. Slocan communities, huddled along the lakeshores, are small now and time battered, quietly going to seed amid the splendors of a mountain landscape. Their heyday has passed — but what a magnificent heyday it was, when silver was king and Slocan mines were booming.

Even today the name Slocan is synonymous with silver, which was as equally alluring as gold in the early 1890s when the bonanzas of the Cariboo had faded. Jim Brennan, prospecting in the rugged Slocan Mountains above Ainsworth in 1889 came across a deposit of galena (a mixture of silver and lead) which assayed out at 150 ounces of silver per ton. When word of this unbelievably rich strike filtered out to the mining world, the rush was on. The lonely mountains of the Slocan swarmed with miners, most of them Americans. In those days, natural transportation routes southwards encouraged a dependence on the U.S. for investment and supplies. The "big town" where miners went to spend their fortunes was not Victoria, which had catered to the Cariboo, but Spokane. And the wildest celebrations of the year were held on the American Fourth of July.

The silver stampede rushed through the Slocan with as much vehemence as the Cariboo gold rush and lasted considerably longer. It was less romantic than the gold rush however, for the minerals needed a lot of capital to extract and transport. It was the era, not of the goldpan and shovel but of the railway, which linked up with paddlewheel steamers on the lakes to bring people and supplies in and ore out of the country. Towns sprang up along the lakes and burgeoned with the new-found wealth, but when the silver market collapsed (in Spokane alone five banks went bankrupt) they settled into a gentle decline. Many of them are ghosts now, while others cling to a shadow of the life they once knew. Around them, the mountains are dotted with spectres of a different sort — mines and machinery, stamp mills and reduction plants, tailings, railway roadbeds, trestles — picturesque only to eyes that can see them as they once were, tinged with the hopeful gleam of silver.

There are several approach routes to the Slocan. You can drive from Castlegar in the south, following the Slocan River and the east shore of Slocan Lake to Silverton and New Denver. You can drop down from Revelstoke on Highway 23, ferry across Upper Arrow Lake and drive down to Nakusp, or you can go over Monashee Pass from the Okanagan Valley at Vernon, then up Lower Arrow Lake. Whatever your route, make New Denver your destination. For this town on Slocan Lake is the start of a backroad that cuts over the Slocan Range of the Selkirks, through the heart of the silver mines and out to Kaslo on Kootenay Lake, a 40-mile trip through history.

New Denver, so named because it was expected to outstrip the glories of Denver, Colorado, was a rip-roaring metropolis at the turn of the century, a spangled town where miners from the rugged bush could indulge themselves in the luxuries of civilization. The Newmarket Hotel, a fine balconied building on the lakefront, was one of the few relics of this era left in the tumbledown town; until it burned down in 1974 it had operated continuously for more than 80 years. The road to Kaslo is well signposted and leads steeply up behind the town for a good view of the lake. Houses give way momentarily to old farmsteads and abandoned orchards before the valley of Seaton Creek becomes a forested canyon, the road etched into its northern flank. About four miles from New Denver, the road forks southeast to Sandon. At the junction, where three creeks converge, once stood the town of Three Forks, a string of hotels and saloons that called itself "the heart of the Slocan" — and lasted a scant 20 years. The undisputed capital of Slocan silver was Sandon, three miles up Carpenter Creek in a steep valley where mountains shoulder out the sun for most of the day.

The mines around here, the richest of them all, were discovered in 1891 by a circus acrobat Eli Carpenter and his partner Jack Seaton who climbed up Payne Mountain to scout out a quicker way to Ainsworth, where the government assayer and mining office were located. On the summit they picked up some samples from a promising outcrop and took them to be assayed. The ore samples proved rich. According to legend, Eli the acrobat tried to double-cross his partner. He showed him assay results from another, worthless claim, meaning to keep the rich Payne deposits for himself and his pals. But Carpenter and his friend Jim Sandon were overheard plotting the scheme; Seaton was told of it, got together a party of five and raced to Payne Mountain, beating Carpenter's group by a day. Seaton staked several rich claims, one of which he named "The Noble Five". This strike precipitated a frantic rush to the area; hundreds of worthwhile claims were staked, and many were good ones. The Slocan Star, the Reco-Goodenough, whose ore yielded over 400 ounces of silver per ton, the Payne Boy, which made a profit of $4 million, and others went down in the annals of mining history.

Amid all this flurry and excitement, Sandon was born. At first it was only another rough mining camp beside Carpenter Creek — places were named after villains as well as heroes, it seems. But in 1892 along came Johnnie Harris who founded a town. Six years later, with a population of more than 2,000, Sandon was granted city status and soon filled all the available space in the narrow valley bottom. Undaunted, the real estate entrepreneurs of the day simply channelled the creek into wooden culverts and diverted the main street of the city over the top, leaving land for more

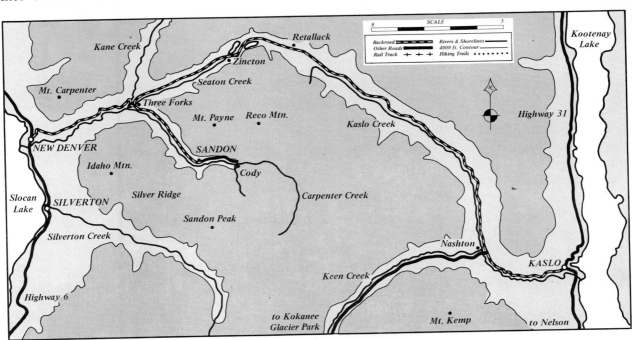

Left: Beavers have flooded some of the old townsite of Zincton and the mining sheds are toppling into the pond. Top: The Zincton concentrator.

Above Left: Steep-roofed log cabin at Whitewater has survived many winters. Above Right: The many-gabled Langham Hotel, one of Kaslo's many mining day relics.

buildings. In its salad days, Sandon boasted 24 hotels and saloons, most with gambling houses attached, a newspaper, the Sandon Paystreak, a grand opera house, a city hall, a brewery, churches, electric lights generated by Johnnie Harris' own hydro-electric plant, the second in the province, and lots of houses, plain and fancy. Sandon was opulent; its hotels had solid oak bedsteads and feather mattresses, the finest porcelain chamber pots, brass spittoons, elaborate bars of polished mahogany, plate-glass mirrors, steam heat and electric bells to summon the chambermaids. Miners gambled and drank and danced six nights of the week, then went to church on Sundays and put their left-over poker chips in the collection plate, a practice gladly accepted by the parson.

Two railways had raced to Sandon to corner the fat ore contracts: the Canadian Pacific hurried to lay steel up from New Denver while the narrow gauge Kaslo & Slocan, an off-shoot of the American Great Northern, rushed around from Kaslo. K&S trainmen arrived in Sandon to find the mighty CPR already there. They were so disappointed that they hitched one of their two wood-burning steam engines to the CPR depot and pulled it into the creek!

In this steep and shadowy valley the gay times were mixed with tragedy. The mines were high in the mountains, reached only by narrow trails (packtrains of horses rawhided the ore down to Sandon) and in winter colossal snowfalls turned the trails to deathtraps. Miners were buried alive by avalanches as they plodded home. The slide area on the trail to the Noble Five mine was a notorious killer, exacting its tolls every year without fail. One Christmas Eve, the slide killed five men returning to Sandon for the festivities.

Fire, the scourge of all mining towns, struck Sandon twice, in 1900 and again six years later. Each time, the city rose again from the ashes, bigger and bolder than ever. It seemed indestructible. But it was only as strong as the mines. When the price of silver slumped and the rich ore veins began petering out, the mines closed, one by one, and people drifted away. There was no sudden exodus. The city lingered for years. Johnnie Harris stayed on with a couple of the old-timers until the 1950s, populating the great empty shell of a place with their memories. But when Harris died in 1953, the ghosts had pretty well taken over.

Today, Sandon bears little trace of its past. In the spring of 1955, the creek which the city fathers had boarded over and which had given the city its glamorous electric light, broke loose from its 50-year-old confines and smashed the town. Foundations were eroded, buildings toppled. The main street was reduced to a gigantic pile of wrecked lumber. Only a few buildings survived the water's fury — the Virginia Block, built of bricks in 1910, the city hall, a store, the small frame courthouse, the K&S station and some of the houses up the sides of the gulch. Sandon today is a ghost town, sadly shattered and forlorn, but enough remains beside the creek to allow a mental reconstruction of past magnificence. Higher up the creek is the ghost town of Cody, once a model town built to house the workers in the Noble Five concentrator. The few relics of mining days still to be found at Cody are of more recent vintage.

From Cody, return down the creek to the site of Three Forks and turn right, following Seaton Creek five miles up to the divide at Zincton (3,530 feet) where mine buildings spill down the hillside in a tumble of green paint and rusty tin roofs. Beavers have taken possession of the townsite and many of the buildings are toppling into newly-formed beaver ponds. Some of the lodges are enormous. The Zincton camp was first staked in 1892, but never amounted to much because zinc was far less precious than silver. In 1903, new owners came in to search for richer ore leads, but their camp was destroyed by a forest fire. Finally, the Victoria Syndicate, who bought control in 1927, decided that zinc was a valuable commodity in its own right and built a huge concentrator to process the ore before shipment. The mine lasted into the 1940s.

Over the divide, Bear Lake and swampy Fish Lake are the headwater sources of Kaslo Creek, which the road follows the rest of the way to Kaslo. After a lazy start in the lakes, the creek, gathering strength from its tributaries, picks up speed and rushes pell-mell through a narrow canyon of black slate, the road clinging on beside it. The foaming fury of the creek suggested the name of Whitewater, the next mining settlement along the road, although later this was changed to Retallack. A million dollars in almost solid galena came from the mines above this town, where once seven hotels, stores, houses, a sawmill, concentrator and powderhouse filled the flats beside the creek. You'll recognize Whitewater by the red-painted frame buildings beside the road, by the ruins of the concentrator and by the old, steep-roofed log cabins in the meadows beside the creek. There are log cabins, too, at Nashton, 12 miles down the road, across the creek on a sturdy log bridge. Nashton came into its own as a shipping centre in 1892 when eight major mines opened up nearby and wealth from such claims as the Montezuma, the Cork-Province and Minnie May's Gibson Mine poured through its streets. A side road leads through Nashton up Keen Creek to the old Joker Mill site (16 miles). Here you must park for the steep hike in to Kokanee Glacier Provincial Park with its handful of fishing lakes. If you plan to park overnight, you must protect your car tires from porcupines which seem to have an insatiable craving for rubber. Two layers of stout chicken wire are needed to keep them at bay.

It's five miles downhill from Nashton to Kaslo on the shore of Kootenay Lake, another mining town that boomed with the mines and is still trying to recover from their loss. Kaslo, end of steel for the little K&S Railway, was the freighting and supply centre for the Slocan mines. It was also the home of peppery old Colonel R.T. Lowery, who started the Kaslo Claim newspaper here, one of eight newspapers he founded in the Kootenays. The claim achieved a kind of notoriety when it printed half-paid advertisements sideways and unpaid ones upside-down. "Silver, lead and hell are

*Above: The shattered relics of
Sandon beside Carpenter
Creek. Opposite Page:
Collection of old ironware
decorates a Sandon shed door.
Right: The New Denver-Kaslo
road, golden trees and a
distant view of the Monashees.*

raised in the Slocan, and unless you can take a hand in producing these articles, your services are not required", Lowery wrote in his paper, which folded after 16 weeks. Kaslo looks back to disaster days — to the great fire which destroyed half the town in 1894, the hurricane a year later which uprooted it again, followed the next day by a flood which carried away the rest of the town. But as long as there was silver in the hills, Kaslo rebuilt and prospered. In 1893 it became an incorporated city, with a population of 1,500 and 20 grand hotels. When the mines declined, Kaslo waned. But today much remains of the old town: the three-storey Langham Hotel with its row of dormer windows; St. Andrew's Church (1893), the city hall (1898), the S.S. Moyie, one of the last of the paddlewheelers on the lake, now safely beached as a museum; streets of gracious, tree-shaded frame houses and a main street with false-fronted shops. Kaslo today is a town to linger in. The view across the lake to the towering peaks of the Purcell Range is fine indeed.

South down the highway some 13 miles on the way to Nelson, lies Ainsworth, the earliest town in the Slocan, founded in 1882 on the site first known as Hot Springs Camp because it was here that local Indians came for curative baths in the sulphur springs. The town rose to prominence with the Slocan mines and was destroyed by the inevitable fire in 1898. Only the balconied Silver Ledge Hotel remains. The hot springs have been turned into a resort. You can wade through the warm water to the source of the springs at the back of a U-shaped cave. Nearby is Cody Cave Provincial Park.

TOUR 25
Kootenay Mission Road

From Cranbrook in the East Kootenays, most travellers head east to see Fort Steele, the recreated town of the gold rush era, complete with police fort, hotels, churches, homes, waterwheels, stage coaches and steam engines. It is one of the tourist sights of the area. But few people know of the historic church of St. Eugene, just a few miles away, and fewer still drive the scenic shortcut route across St. Mary's River.

If you are driving down from Radium along Highway 95, take the alternative route that branches right to Kimberley through Ta Ta Creek. Five miles beyond the junction, just past Kimberley Airport, the highway makes a right-angled bend to the right (west) and a gravel road continues due south. This is the start of the mission backroad. Follow the road over a cattleguard into a marshy area, reeded and bushy, with little boggy lakes, a favorite nesting area of Eastern kingbirds in the spring. Then the road climbs into pinewoods, the haunt of Mariposa lilies and wild nodding onion, interspersed with homestead clearings. At the five-mile mark, where the road angles to the left, you come to a sign denoting the start of Indian Reserve No. 1. From here to the river you're in the lands of the Kootenay Indians, so do not stray off the road without permission.

Continue through the Indian woodlands and take the right-hand branch of a prominent forks. This will lead eventually into a large unfenced meadow, like a golden island in the middle of a pine-wood sea where, above the dark thrusts of evergreens you can see the red rock needles of the surrounding mountains. In the meadow scores of meadowlarks make their home, enriching the air with their songs. Soon afterwards, the road descends steeply to the valley of St. Mary's River, joining a wider road that runs beside it. From the top of the bluffs you can look across to the red roofs of the mission on the opposite shore.

To reach the mission, turn right and head upriver a short distance to the bridge. But before you do, drive downstream a way to see the eroded clay cliffs of the escarpment. In places there are arched indentations that remind one of the cliff dwellings of Colorado's famed Mesa Verde. The river is wide and swift, fed by glaciers in the high Purcell Mountains. Upriver, it is joined by four tributaries named Matthew, Mark, Luke and John by one of the Oblate missionaries.

Return now and cross the river to the mission of St. Eugene. Founded in 1874 by the Oblates where St. Joseph's Creek flows into the river, it was an outpost of civilization in the Kootenay wilderness long before Cranbrook was even surveyed. There was a residential school here as early as 1890 and a few years later, a 40-bed hospital was built. This cared for the victims of the typhoid epidemic that swept the country when the Crows Nest Pass Railway was a building. From the very start, the mission had to be self sufficient. There was a fine farm where the missionaries grew wheat and vegetables and ran livestock, and they ground their own flour in a home-made mill.

The church on the opposite side of the road from the massive three-storey school, is one of the

Opposite Page: The mission church of St. Eugene in a meadow of flowering gumweed. Left: Sandstone pinnacles and caves above St. Mary's River. Below: Wild delphiniums and thistles, typical dry country blooms.

finest wooden churches of its era in B.C., and one of the oldest. Its ornate steeple rises proudly against the rim of rocky mountains to the east. The church is interesting historically as well as architecturally, for it was built from the proceeds of a silver mine. The year was 1893 and Father Coccola tried to encourage his Indian parishioners to search for minerals. He showed them samples of ore-bearing rock, calling them "chickamon" or money stones. After a while, disappointed in their lack of interest, he forgot about the project.

Then in stalked Pierre, an Indian who had once threatened Father Coccola's life. He threw down a rock heavy with ore, but at first would not say where he found it. The assayer reported almost solid galena (a mixture of silver and lead) and offered to buy the rich claim, sight unseen. James Cronin, a Spokane mining man staying at the mission, Father Coccola and Pierre set off to the site of Pierre's discovery, a steep hillside above Moyie Lake, southwest of St. Eugene. Father Coccola and Pierre staked two claims and Cronin returned later to stake a third. Cronin raised money in the U.S. to develop the mine and the other two sold their claims to the company for $22,000.

The money was used to build a church at Moyie, the settlement that sprang up at the foot of the new mine, and also to build what Father Coccola called his "beautiful Gothic church" of St. Eugene at the mission, the church that is standing there today. Pierre, it is said, was given a new house on the reserve and a pension for life. But rumor has it that inside his new white man's house Pierre put up his old tepee, cutting a hole through the roof of the house to let out the smoke from his fire.

From the mission, follow the road south along St. Joseph's Creek to join Highway 95A again just before Cranbrook. If you are heading back to Vancouver along Highway 3, you will pass through Moyie, a ramshackle little town today, beside the lake. High on the hillside above is the outcrop where Pierre found his lump of galena — and built a church. The mine, once one of the richest in the Kootenays, is no longer worked.

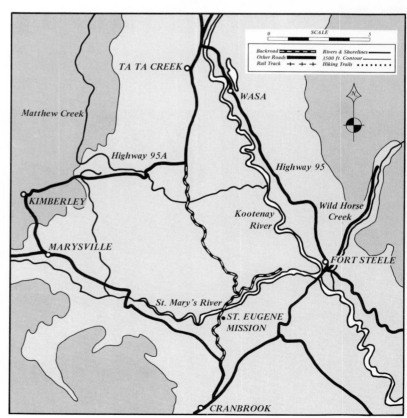

Bibliography

Akrigg, G.P.V. and Helen: 1001 B.C. Place Names; Discovery Press, 1969.

Balf, Mary: Kamloops, A History of the District up to 1914.

Barlee, N.L.: Canada West Magazine; Gold Creeks and Ghost Towns; The Guide to Gold Panning in British Columbia.

Boundary Historical Society, Reports.

Choate, Avis L.: The Clinton Story.

Clark, Lewis: Wild Flowers of British Columbia, Gray's Publishing Ltd.

Corner, John: Pictographs in the Interior of B.C.

Cronin, Kay: Cross in the Wilderness, Mitchell Press Ltd.

Downs, Art: Paddlewheels on the Frontier, Gray's Publishing, Sidney. Wagon Road North, Northwest Digest Ltd.

Downs, Art, ed.: Pioneer Days in B.C. Volumes I and II, Foremost Publishing Co.Ltd.

Frontier Guide: The Dewdney Trail, Three volumes, Frontier Publishing Ltd.

Garman, E.H.: Pocket Guide to the Trees and Shrubs of British Columbia, B.C. Forest Service.

Godman, Josephine: Pioneer Days of Port Renfrew, Solitaire Publications.

Graham, Clara: This was the Kootenay.

Hearn, George and Wilkie, David: The Cordwood Ltd, B.C. Railway Historical Association.

Hutchison, Bruce: The Fraser, Clarke, Irwin & Co.Ltd.

Kay, Dave, ed: Come with me to Yesterday.

Lazeo, L.: Collector's Guide to B.C. Artifacts Sites.

Leaming, S.: Rock and Mineral Collecting in B.C., Dept. of Energy.

Lee, Norman: Klondike Cattle Drive, Mitchell Press.

Lindsay, F.W.: The Cariboo Story; Cariboo Yarns; The Outlaws.

Lyons, C.P.: Milestones on the Mighty Fraser; Milestones in Ogopogo Land; Trees, Flowers and Shrubs to know in B.C., Dent.

Merriman, Alex and Taffy: Logging Road Travel, Saltaire Publishing Ltd.

Okanagan Historical Society, Reports.

Ormsby, Margaret: British Columbia, a History, MacMillan of Canada.

Pattison, Ken: Milestones on Vancouver Island, Milestone Publications.

Pethick, Derek; Victoria The Fort, Mitchell Press Ltd.

Ramsey, Bruce; Ghost Towns of British Columbia, Mitchell Press, 1963.

Rodgers, John: The Birds of Vancouver, Bryan Publications Ltd.; Shorebirds and Predators, J.J. Douglas.

Ronayne, Irene: Beyond Garibaldi, Lillooet Publishers.

Rothenburger, Mel: "We've killed Johnny Ussher", Mitchell Press Ltd.

Scott, David and Hanic, Edna: East Kootenay Saga, Nunaga Publishing Co.Ltd.

Shewchuk, Murphy and Sandra: Exploring Kamloops Country, Peerless Printers Ltd.

Stanley, George F.G. ed.: Mapping the Frontier between B.C. and Washington, MacMillan of Canada.

Wright, Richard and Rochelle: Cariboo Mileposts, Mitchell Press.

Index